A Carolina Psalter

A Carolina Psalter

by
Tony Scully

RESOURCE *Publications* · Eugene, Oregon

A CAROLINA PSALTER

Copyright © 2019 Tony Scully. All rights reserved. Except for brief quotations in critical publications or reviews, no part of this book may be reproduced in any manner without prior written permission from the publisher. Write: Permissions, Wipf and Stock Publishers, 199 W. 8th Ave., Suite 3, Eugene, OR 97401.

Resource Publications
An Imprint of Wipf and Stock Publishers
199 W. 8th Ave., Suite 3
Eugene, OR 97401

www.wipfandstock.com

PAPERBACK ISBN: 978-1-7252-5140-3
HARDCOVER ISBN: 978-1-7252-5141-0
EBOOK ISBN: 978-1-7252-5142-7

Manufactured in the U.S.A.   NOVEMBER 1, 2019

For the Psalms, I chose The American Standard Version (ASV) for its language and its remarkable history. The ASV is in universal public domain. The ASV is rooted in the Revised Version (RV), a 19th-century British revision of the King James Version of 1611. In 1870, an invitation was extended to American religious leaders for scholars to work on the RV project. A year later, Protestant theologian Philip Schaff chose 30 scholars representing the denominations of Baptist, Congregationalist, Dutch Reformed, Friends, Methodist, Episcopal, Presbyterian, Protestant Episcopal, and Unitarian. The ASV is the basis of the Revised Standard Version, 1971, the Amplified Bible, 1965, the New American Standard Bible, 1995, and the Recovery Version, 1999. A fifth revision, known as the World English Bible, was published in 2000 and was placed in the public domain. Note: where advisable, I changed the word, "Jehovah," to "God," to reflect common usage.
For the poems, *A Carolina Psalter* by Anthony Patrick Scully is registered with the Library of Congress. Registration Number: TXu 2-116-370

to Joy Claussen

Good Wife and Star

> You shine within us, outside us—even darkness shines—when we remember
> —*The Lord's Prayer*, translated from the Aramaic

Contents

Preface | xi
Acknowledgements | xiii
Introduction | xv

Psalm One | 1
Psalm Two | 3
Psalm Three | 5
Psalm Four | 7
Psalm Five | 9
Psalm Six | 12
Psalm Seven | 14
Psalm Eight | 17
Psalm Nine | 19
Psalm Ten | 22
Psalm Eleven | 26
Psalm Twelve | 28
Psalm Thirteen | 30
Psalm Fourteen | 32
Psalm Fifteen | 34
Psalm Sixteen | 36
Psalm Seventeen | 38
Psalm Eighteen | 41
Psalm Nineteen | 47
Psalm Twenty | 49
Psalm Twenty-one | 51
Psalm Twenty-two | 53
Psalm Twenty-three | 57
Psalm Twenty-four | 59
Psalm Twenty-five | 61
Psalm Twenty-six | 64
Psalm Twenty-seven | 66
Psalm Twenty-eight | 69
Psalm Twenty-nine | 71
Psalm Thirty | 73
Psalm Thirty-one | 75
Psalm Thirty-two | 78
Psalm Thirty-three | 80
Psalm Thirty-four | 83
Psalm Thirty-five | 86
Psalm Thirty-six | 89
Psalm Thirty-seven | 91
Psalm Thirty-eight | 95
Psalm Thirty-nine | 98
Psalm Forty | 100
Psalm Forty-one | 103
Psalm Forty-two | 106
Psalm Forty-three | 108
Psalm Forty-four | 110
Psalm Forty-five | 113
Psalm Forty-six | 116
Psalm Forty-seven | 118
Psalm Forty-eight | 120
Psalm Forty-nine | 122
Psalm Fifty | 125
Psalm Fifty-one | 128
Psalm Fifty-two | 131
Psalm Fifty-three | 133
Psalm Fifty-four | 135
Psalm Fifty-five | 137

Psalm Fifty-six | 140
Psalm Fifty-seven | 143
Psalm Fifty-eight | 145
Psalm Fifty-nine | 147
Psalm Sixty | 150
Psalm Sixty-one | 153
Psalm Sixty-two | 155
Psalm Sixty-three | 157
Psalm Sixty-four | 159
Psalm Sixty-five | 161
Psalm Sixty-six | 164
Psalm Sixty-seven | 167
Psalm Sixty-eight | 169
Psalm Sixty-nine | 173
Psalm Seventy | 177
Psalm Seventy-one | 179
Psalm Seventy-two | 182
Psalm Seventy-three | 185
Psalm Seventy-four | 189
Psalm Seventy-five | 192
Psalm Seventy-six | 194
Psalm Seventy-seven | 196
Psalm Seventy-eight | 199
Psalm Seventy-nine | 205
Psalm Eighty | 207
Psalm Eighty-one | 210
Psalm Eighty-two | 212
Psalm Eighty-three | 214
Psalm Eighty-four | 216
Psalm Eighty-five | 218
Psalm Eighty-six | 220
Psalm Eighty-seven | 223
Psalm Eighty-eight | 225

Psalm Eighty-nine | 227
Psalm Ninety | 232
Psalm Ninety-one | 234
Psalm Ninety-two | 236
Psalm Ninety-three | 239
Psalm Ninety-four | 241
Psalm Ninety-five | 244
Psalm Ninety-six | 246
Psalm Ninety-seven | 248
Psalm Ninety-eight | 250
Psalm Ninety-nine | 252
Psalm One hundred | 254
Psalm One hundred one | 255
Psalm One hundred two | 257
Psalm One hundred three | 260
Psalm One hundred four | 263
Psalm One hundred five | 267
Psalm One hundred six | 271
Psalm One hundred seven | 276
Psalm One hundred eight | 280
Psalm One hundred nine | 282
Psalm One hundred ten | 286
Psalm One hundred eleven | 288
Psalm One hundred twelve | 290
Psalm One hundred thirteen | 292
Psalm One hundred fourteen | 294
Psalm One hundred fifteen | 296
Psalm One hundred sixteen | 299
Psalm One hundred seventeen | 301
Psalm One hundred eighteen | 302
Psalm One hundred nineteen | 305
Psalm One hundred twenty | 318
Psalm One hundred twenty-one | 320

Psalm One hundred twenty-two | 321
Psalm One hundred twenty-three | 323
Psalm One hundred twenty-four | 325
Psalm One hundred twenty-five | 327
Psalm One hundred twenty-six | 329
Psalm One hundred twenty-seven | 331
Psalm One hundred twenty-eight | 333
Psalm One hundred twenty-nine | 335
Psalm One hundred thirty | 337
Psalm One hundred thirty-one | 339
Psalm One hundred thirty-two | 341
Psalm One hundred thirty-three | 344
Psalm One hundred thirty-four | 345
Psalm One hundred thirty-five | 346
Psalm One hundred thirty-six | 349
Psalm One hundred thirty-seven | 352
Psalm One hundred thirty-eight | 354
Psalm One hundred thirty-nine | 356
Psalm One hundred forty | 359
Psalm One hundred forty-one | 361
Psalm One hundred forty-two | 363
Psalm One hundred forty-three | 365
Psalm One hundred forty-four | 368
Psalm One hundred forty-five | 371
Psalm One hundred forty-six | 373
Psalm One hundred forty-seven | 375
Psalm One hundred forty-eight | 378
Psalm One hundred forty-nine | 380
Psalm One hundred fifty | 382

About the Author | 383

Preface

In the tumultuous spirit of the American South, *A Carolina Psalter* offers an outspoken conversation with King David's Psalms, great outcries to a personal God. The Psalms, as a transformational work, sing out in the confident voice of a people unafraid to address the deity almost as an equal, and in some cases, as a friend. The poems in *A Carolina Psalter* address the God of the Psalms with questioning, irreverence, and occasional confrontation as we move into new understandings of Spirit. If we wish, we can experience the Psalms, indeed all the Bible, as living poetry, its metaphors breathing vibrant new life into our souls. Tony Scully's poems challenge what he calls "the war God of tradition," often questioning whether that God, so often on the front lines of revenge and destroying one's enemies, if not altogether absent during periods of loss and disaster, can possibly be God at all. His poems, although reflecting current thought and practice concerning the omnipresence of Spirit, spring from a well-founded history of believers, indeed, from the Bible itself, acknowledging the divine presence within. They assert the authority of the individual voice in a search for a God beyond accepted boundaries and definitions.

Acknowledgements

Thank you to the following people for their assistance with the publication of *A Carolina Psalter*: to my wife, Joy Claussen Scully for her constant support; to Richard Brown, Director of the University of South Carolina Press, who put me in touch with Wipf & Stock; to the Reverend Dr. William F. ("Chip") Summers for his infinite wisdom in all matters secular and profane; to Marty Daniels for her unerring eye and typical good judgment, especially with my Introduction; to Earl Bryant, MD for his sense of reality after a lifetime of practicing medicine; to Drew Casper, PhD, University of Southern California School of Cinematic Arts for his enthusiasm for my work, even for my worst instincts; to Nina ffrench-Frazier von Eckardt, critic extraordinaire; to Ponza and Robert Vaughan, the best of friends and readers.

Introduction

With *A Carolina Psalter* and my poems in conversation with the Psalms, I felt it was time to speak. The Psalms, some of them almost 2500 years old, have been with us in the Judeo-Christian tradition in every worship service, every prayer meeting, and every Mass for generation upon generation, their lyrical beauty manifest. As we become increasingly fixated on nuclear weapons and armaments, however, we cannot avoid inevitable questions. Why are we constantly at war? Even as we pray in good faith, do we pray to a war god? If God is our bulwark, as the Psalms maintain, why are so many of the best of us addicted to fighting? Why so much gun violence? Why so much addiction? Why so many suicides? Who is this God the Bible presents to us?

The pervasive kindness of believers in small towns and cities across the American South suggests they are deeply touched by Scripture. From prayers to the Heavenly Father and group discussions about Jesus come armies of compassionate, world-serving people who serve the homeless, the hungry, the grieving, and the incarcerated with warm hearts and the best of intentions. For many others, however, the Bible sets forth outmoded or impossible absolutes, from injunctions about the place of women and slaves, to the doctrine that Jesus is divine, to the imperative that we destroy our enemies.

Literal interpretation of the Bible may be the least of it. The argument is not about whether Eve ate a literal apple with a literal snake beside her, or whether Noah really built an ark. The question is about God. Who is this being? What is the nature of God? Many of the most progressive minds on the planet hardly believe in Spirit at all. Others address a Father God. Why is God a Father, a sometimes-threatening term for many, even if Jesus called him that? Others argue for God as Mind or Creative Source. Whole theologies, perhaps not intentionally, describe a spiritual universe predicated on good versus evil: the forces of light versus the forces of darkness. These interpretations run deep in our DNA and show up in our prayers and in our Scripture. In many cases, this duality seems to underpin and reinforce well-intentioned theological thinking—feeding into national and international conflicts and unrest, as in "God is on our side."

We are increasingly a nation at war. Extended wars. We are four percent of the world's population; we spend more money on defense than the next ten countries combined. Are we creating yet another empire? Where are we going? And who is this God of the Psalms that seems to be in the thick of it, savaging our enemies? Yes, we do pray, "the Lord is my shepherd," surely a more benign presence, but he would seem insufficient for the argument. His alter ego, like unto Zeus, seems to dominate the proceedings.

As a young man, I became a Jesuit when I joined the Society of Jesus, an event that set me on an almost unending spiritual quest. The Jesuits, then as now, were committed to social justice and to scholarship, which is not to say every denomination, religious order, congregation, and sect does not embrace its own philosophies about what galvanized its founders; namely, the worship of God as they understood God. The Calvinists, as one example, following their understanding of God, are passionate about building a better and more equitable Earth. We are not so different.

The advancing conservatism in the Catholic Church in the seventies and eighties effectively closed down open-minded theological scholarship and discussion in American Catholic colleges and universities. During that period, when an almost ferocious evangelical movement seemed determined to influence local and national politics, the question, "Who is God?" sounded almost heretical. Believers knew for sure who God was. If the Bible didn't tell them so, they knew absolutely that the Holy Spirit was the guiding presence in the Christian church and family. Even the most hidebound understood the commonality of the different Christian communities and were beginning to open themselves to the idea that non-Christians were worshipping the same God.

For some of us, self-professed spiritualists in an emerging culture of non-belief, especially in Manhattan, where I lived for many years, it seemed a truism that if the Bible was revealed truth, so were Mozart and Bach and Beethoven and Henri Matisse and Shakespeare, not to mention Einstein and Nikola Tesla and Thomas Edison and about a million other creative people who somehow channeled new visions and new understanding of the universe, continually unlocking what had been called "the secrets" in physics, chemistry, and biology. Talk to any composer; he or she might tell you they serve as vehicles for energies that come through them, from where they are never sure. I remember a literary agent many years ago, no doubt in flight from some kind of orthodoxy, who ridiculed that idea outright: "Channeling—what a fanciful superstition"! But she wasn't a composer, was she?

In the early seventies, still a Jesuit, after my three years at the Yale School of Drama, where I also served as a deacon for the Reverend William Sloane Coffin Jr., as well as being Writer in Residence at Joseph Papp's Public Theatre one year, I worked for five years as Project Director of the Jesuit-sponsored Woodstock Center for Religion and Worship, no connection to the rock festival, at the Interchurch Center, 475 Riverside Drive, New York. Its mission was the exploration and renewal of liturgy in collaboration with such leading anthropologists, sociologists, psychologists, and theologians as Rollo May and Jungian Edward C. Whitmont. Dr. Whitmont, a former colleague of Carl Jung, spoke about the revelation of personal and collective truth in dreams and trance states. He had also experienced his patients in group therapy dreaming the same dreams. He spoke of patients reexperiencing trauma from past lives. In short, the language of belief was expanding before us. During that time, I also wrote a series of Prayers of the Faithful for Benziger Brothers, a liturgical press that offered contemporary language to the Prayers of the Faithful for the Youth Mass, as it was called. The prayers invoked everyone from John Lennon to Billie Holiday and Nelson Mandela. The idea was to stimulate like-minded language and thinking—to open up windows and doors to the world, especially the world of creativity, often in a surrounding landscape of suffering and violence. My thinking even then, aligned with Martin Luther's idea that all believers were priests.

Once again, the question loomed: Who decides what voices come from God? Who draws the line between the secular and the profane? One might as well ask who has the authority to recognize love. Are we so blinded by the horrors of the twentieth century that we cannot see the light in the darkness?

By the time I left the Society of Jesus after 14 years in 1973, a prominent theologian made the public comment that what believers shared in common were not doctrinal certainties or any clear definition of God, but that in an age of increasing non-belief we were asking the eternal questions—and the questions said it all: "Who is God? Who are we in relation to God? What happens when we die"? The operative point: how could any belief system pin down God? You'd have to be arrogant or stupid to think so.

In the beginning of my new life outside the institutional Church, I chose not to be ordained a priest. The gulf between my personal beliefs and the official teaching had grown too wide. Since then, after a lifetime of questioning, I embrace all religions with love and reverence and take orders from none.

Today, my wife, Joy, and I live in South Carolina. As mayor of a small city here I spent many hours in many churches, especially at funerals and anniversary services praising the name of God. The South is a culture of hymns and blessings. As we press forward with our exuberant spirits in this extraordinary place, we also live with ghosts. If we listen carefully, we can hear the shouts and cries from the Indian wars, the American Revolution, the Civil War, and feel the sorrows of the enslaved.

My journey into the mysteries of spiritual awareness has been a long one and continues to open into the future. I wrote *A Carolina Psalter* for people who are looking to know God, as I am, a God who cannot be reduced to anthropological identity, a God, if you will, beyond gods, a God almost beyond understanding—beyond ritual and inherited prayer, a God of a trillion stars and planets, who we have been told by his prophets lives in our simple hearts as the God of love. Let us hope.

A Carolina Psalter—but one voice. Read the Psalms. Read the poems. Then, speak in your own voice. Share what comes to you. We will listen.

Psalm One

1 Blessed is the man that walketh not in the counsel of the wicked,
Nor standeth in the way of sinners,
Nor sitteth in the seat of scoffers:
² But his delight is in the law of God;
And on his law doth he meditate day and night.
³ And he shall be like a tree planted by the streams of water,
That bringeth forth its fruit in its season,
Whose leaf also doth not wither;
And whatsoever he doeth shall prosper.
⁴ The wicked are not so,
But are like the chaff which the wind driveth away.
⁵ Therefore the wicked shall not stand in the judgment,
Nor sinners in the congregation of the righteous.
⁶ For God knoweth the way of the righteous;
But the way of the wicked shall perish.

Have a blessed day, we say
Blessed be me for not walking in step with the wicked
That be the invocation.
That be the deal

What fool can say she or he is not depraved?
We draw pride from our arsenal
We do
Blessed be our nuclear bombs
Our missile defenses
Protecting us as You never could
Or would
Gospoodi pomiluj
And
Inshallah
Yes Sir

We ourselves could be the enemy
Blessed be the one who meditates on You
Night and day
Feasting on Clozaril
Olanzapine
Flupentixol

We are like trees planted by streams
Our destiny to bear fruit

We pray
The sun not disappear
Or the stream change course
Our delight lies in being alive
Open to sunlight
And laughter

Contradictions
And questioning
At our very core

That's what we say

We do

Psalm Two

1 Why do the nations rage,
And the peoples meditate a vain thing?
² The kings of the earth set themselves,
And the rulers take counsel together,
Against God, and against his anointed, saying,
³ Let us break their bonds asunder,
And cast away their cords from us.
⁴ He that sitteth in the heavens will laugh:
The Lord will have them in derision.
⁵ Then will he speak unto them in his wrath,
And vex them in his sore displeasure:
⁶ Yet I have set my king
Upon my holy hill of Zion.
⁷ I will tell of the decree:
God said unto me, Thou art my son;
This day have I begotten thee.
⁸ Ask of me, and I will give thee the nations for thine inheritance,
And the uttermost parts of the earth for thy possession.
⁹ Thou shalt break them with a rod of iron;
Thou shalt dash them in pieces like a potter's vessel.
¹⁰ Now therefore be wise, O ye kings:
Be instructed, ye judges of the earth.
¹¹ Serve God with fear,
And rejoice with trembling.
¹² Kiss the son, lest he be angry, and ye perish in the way,
For his wrath will soon be kindled.
Blessed are all they that take refuge in him.

We are surrounded by conspiracy
Everywhere unknown creatures plot to kill
Check the Internet
Facebook

Instagram
Kings and would-be kings
Wannabe rulers and tribes
Hire fools
To demoralize the powerful
That's us
As the Lord, whoever you are today
Has installed them on his holy mountain

Six Flags Magic Mountain?

Where are you now?
Who is this Lord?
Zeus again?
Yahweh? Is that still you?
You bestow on your believers
All the nations of the world
Is that your guarantee?

You will break the leaders
Who violate your laws you say?

How is Herr Hitler and the rest of the despots?
And Papa Joe? How is he?
Mao? Pol Pot?
Destroyed no doubt
With a hundred million of your most devout
The Sanctified
Who died extoling your Holy Name

Psalm Three

1 God, how are mine adversaries increased!
Many are they that rise up against me.
² Many there are that say of my soul,
There is no help for him in God.
³ But thou, O God, art a shield about me;
My glory, and the lifter up of my head.
⁴ I cry unto God with my voice,
And he answereth me out of his holy hill.
⁵ I laid me down and slept;
I awaked; for God sustaineth me.
⁶ I will not be afraid of ten thousands of the people
That have set themselves against me round about.
⁷ Arise, O God; save me, O my God:
For thou hast smitten all mine enemies upon the cheek bone;
Thou hast broken the teeth of the wicked.
⁸ Salvation belongeth unto God:
Thy blessing be upon thy people.

W ho waits in the dark
Plotting against me
Or does darkness do that
By itself?

In the black pit of my mind
The voices are laughing
No one will save me
From death
Not even You
Whoever You are

I call out
Help
To the holy mountain
And I hear
Noise

The world is created
By the vibration of sound
And fury
Or so they say

Now I lay me down to sleep
Will I awake
With a rifle in my ribs
"Get up!"

You wonder why I dream of fire
Intercontinental ballistic missiles
Blowing up
My enemies
Anyone who will sell me
For ten cents on the dollar
And they will

Break the teeth of the wicked
Says the Psalm
Mash the brains
Fry the faces
Erase the histories

Deliver me O Lord
From this darkness you have made
This darkness
That is me

Psalm Four

1 Answer me when I call, O God of my righteousness;
Thou hast set me at large when I was in distress:
Have mercy upon me, and hear my prayer.
² O ye sons of men, how long shall my glory be turned into dishonor?
How long will ye love vanity, and seek after falsehood? Selah
³ But know that God hath set apart for himself him that is godly:
God will hear when I call unto him.
⁴ Stand in awe, and sin not:
Commune with your own heart upon your bed, and be still. Selah
⁵ Offer the sacrifices of righteousness,
And put your trust in God.
⁶ Many there are that say, Who will show us any good?
God, lift thou up the light of thy countenance upon us.
⁷ Thou hast put gladness in my heart,
More than they have when their grain
And their new wine are increased.
⁸ In peace will I both lay me down and sleep;
For thou, God, alone makest me dwell in safety.

The directions say
Play stringed instruments
Violins, violas, cellos, yo guitars

Answer me when I call to You

Hello?

I shout and no one answers
Except myself
Have mercy on me

Who am I talking to?
While the world
Worships currency

Assets
Equities

Who pays for the roof over a newborn's head?

How can I tell my friends
To search their hearts
And be silent
To trust in the world
It's going to be alright
No, Ma'am
It's going to be more waiting
More death
More suffering
Which only brings wisdom they say
The wisdom to know
We do not control a single thing
We can only meditate
On the stillness that is You
And know
Even with nothing
We are not alone
We are blessed
With silence
And with nothingness

And violins

Psalm Five

1 Give ear to my words, O God,
Consider my meditation.
² Hearken unto the voice of my cry, my King, and my God;
For unto thee do I pray.
³ O God, in the morning shalt thou hear my voice;
In the morning will I order my prayer unto thee, and will keep watch.
⁴ For thou art not a God that hath pleasure in wickedness:
Evil shall not sojourn with thee.
⁵ The arrogant shall not stand in thy sight:
Thou hatest all workers of iniquity.
⁶ Thou wilt destroy them that speak lies:
God abhorreth the blood-thirsty and deceitful man.
⁷ But as for me, in the abundance of thy loving
Kindness will I come into thy house:
In thy fear will I worship toward thy holy temple.
⁸ Lead me, O God, in thy righteousness because of mine enemies;
Make thy way straight before my face.
⁹ For there is no faithfulness in their mouth;
Their inward part in every wickedness;
Their throat is an open sepulchre;
They flatter with their tongue.
¹⁰ Hold them guilty, O God;
Let them fall by their own counsels;
Thrust them out in the multitude of their transgressions;
For they have rebelled against thee.
¹¹ But let all those that take refuge in thee rejoice,
Let them ever shout for joy, because thou defendest them:
Let them also that love thy name be joyful in thee.
¹² For thou wilt bless the righteous;
O God, thou wilt compass him with favor as with a shield.

Do I ever stop
Crying out for help

In my dirge
Desperate for a god
Who is only talked about
By people looking for a sovereign ruler
And finding none
Especially in themselves?

I pray for prosperity
What else?

Money the source of all evil
And everything else
Especially shrimp 'n grits
And beachfront property
Is that so?

Is there something wrong with an Escalade
Or a vacation home in St. Tropez
Or will your hurricanes
Destroy that too?

Am I so arrogant
So filled with hate
That the universe is no longer comfortable with me
At least
Not since I began to speak?

I still bow down to tabernacles
Especially the baroque
And recite rosaries at funerals
Along with the devout
And utter Under God
When I pledge allegiance to the flag

And indivisible

They buy and sell the working class
The out-of-working class
And the high fructose
Incapacitated class
Going mad

With dementia and Diabetes II

What do you plan to do with us?
O God, whoever you are
Wherever you hide
We clearly cannot save ourselves

Surely, Lord, you bless the righteous
Do you?
Who are they?
Democrat or Republican?

Have mercy on me
The unknowing
Uncomprehending
Brain Dead
Me

Deliver me
Accept the prayers
Of one drowning in the dark
Weak from the sorrow of the world

And when you think of it

Destroy the destroyers too

In Jesus name, Amen

Psalm Six

1 O God, rebuke me not in thine anger,
Neither chasten me in thy hot displeasure.
² Have mercy upon me, O God; for I am withered away:
O God, heal me; for my bones are troubled.
³ My soul also is sore troubled:
And thou, O God, how long?
⁴ Return, O God, deliver my soul:
Save me for thy loving kindness' sake.
⁵ For in death there is no remembrance of thee:
In Sheol who shall give thee thanks?
⁶ I am weary with my groaning;
Every night make I my bed to swim;
I water my couch with my tears.
⁷ Mine eye wasteth away because of grief;
It waxeth old because of all mine adversaries.
⁸ Depart from me, all ye workers of iniquity;
For God hath heard the voice of my weeping.
⁹ God hath heard my supplication;
God will receive my prayer.
¹⁰ All mine enemies shall be put to shame and sore troubled:
They shall turn back, they shall be put to shame suddenly.

Lord, who am I talking to?

I beg you
Do not rebuke me in your anger
I am the one rebuking me

I tell you my bones are in agony
You or someone else not you
Tells me to see the
Orthopedic surgeon
Or maybe a neurologist

Like a wife abused
Beaten, raped, reviled
I have given up waiting on your name
Knowing it's only a matter of time
Before I too
Am delivered to the flames
My ashes scattered to the winds

Have you given birth to my soul
To let me drown in the dark of the world?
Have you encouraged multiple creeds
So believers can kill and maim
In your name
And drag me into madness
Imprinting on my newborn soul
Tribe as Higher Power?

My analyst takes notes
For the revelation
That I am acting out
With anger
And resentment
And fury
For being alive

Apparently

I no longer wait on a Messiah
Only for the Garden of Eden to return
At least in my imagination
Dancing girls
With incredible legs
And breasts that bounce
To intoxicate me
And mesmerize me
And love me
More than you

Or do I want to be worshipped too?

Psalm Seven

1 O God my God, in thee do I take refuge:
Save me from all them that pursue me, and deliver me,
² Lest they tear my soul like a lion,
Rending it in pieces, while there is none to deliver.
³ O God my God, if I have done this;
If there be iniquity in my hands;
⁴ If I have rewarded evil unto him that was at peace with me
(Yea, I have delivered him that without cause was mine adversary;)
⁵ Let the enemy pursue my soul, and overtake it;
Yea, let him tread my life down to the earth,
And lay my glory in the dust.
⁶ Arise, O God, in thine anger;
Lift up thyself against the rage of mine adversaries,
And awake for me; thou hast commanded judgment.
⁷ And let the congregation of the peoples compass thee about;
And over them return thou on high.
⁸ God ministereth judgment to the peoples:
Judge me, O God, according to my righteousness,
And to mine integrity that is in me.
⁹ Oh let the wickedness of the wicked come to an end,
But establish thou the righteous:
For the righteous God trieth the minds and hearts.
¹⁰ My shield is with God,
Who saveth the upright in heart.
¹¹ God is a righteous judge,
Yea, a God that hath indignation every day.
¹² If a man turn not, he will whet his sword;
He hath bent his bow, and made it ready;
¹³ He hath also prepared for him the instruments of death;
He maketh his arrows fiery shafts.
¹⁴ Behold, he travaileth with iniquity;
Yea, he hath conceived mischief, and brought forth falsehood.
¹⁵ He hath made a pit, and digged it,

And is fallen into the ditch which he made.
¹⁶ His mischief shall return upon his own head,
And his violence shall come down upon his own pate.
¹⁷ I will give thanks unto God according to his righteousness,
And will sing praise to the name of God Most High.

Lordy Lordy
Let's talk about you
The center of imagination
The self-styled creative source
The purported mind
Of the Universe

The world is closing in
I don't envisage enemies
But they carry Kalashnikovs
And plant land mines under my feet
They bring poison into parks and restaurants
To smother and burn and tear us apart

And where be you?

Father forgive them
Is that it?
Will you let them trample me?
Make me sleep in the dust
Then tell me to turn the other cheek?
Where is your anger against my enemies?

I have given alms to the needy
Fed the hungry
Clothed the naked
Or at least written checks
And you let them deliver me
Into the crematoria

They call you a righteous judge
Is that so?

I search my heart to discover
If I am surfeited with despair
Overflowing with evil
And disillusionment

Do I blame the world
For my madness and my gloom?

In the meantime
Praising the God I do not know
I sing the name of the Most High
Just in case
I would prove a fool
To make you mine enemy
Praise God from whom all blessings flow

Yes Ma'am

Psalm Eight

1 O God, our Lord, How excellent is thy name in all the earth,
Who hast set thy glory upon the heavens!
² Out of the mouth of babes and sucklings
Hast thou established strength,
Because of thine adversaries,
That thou mightest still the enemy and the avenger.
³ When I consider thy heavens, the work of thy fingers,
The moon and the stars, which thou hast ordained;
⁴ What is man, that thou art mindful of him?
And the son of man, that thou visitest him?
⁵ For thou hast made him but little lower than God,
And crownest him with glory and honor.
⁶ Thou makest him to have dominion over the works of thy hands;
Thou hast put all things under his feet:
⁷ All sheep and oxen,
Yea, and the beasts of the field,
⁸ The birds of the heavens, and the fish of the sea,
Whatsoever passeth through the paths of the seas.
⁹ O God, our Lord,
How excellent is thy name in all the earth!

Lord, Lord
How majestic your name in all the earth!
Lord, how impossible a term
For anyone who's labored under lords
And examined the experience
Nothing could be more human and more corrupt
Than what passes for nobility

Do you truly want praise?
And worship?
Why is that?
Would you not rather we be
The beings you have made?

Something does not add up here

When we consider your heavens
The work of your hands
The moon and the stars
The Milky Way
Trillions of stars they say
Nothing compares to our DNA
Yet we are incomplete
Damaged masterworks
What exactly did you have in mind?
What is the end game here?

We used to be told
You made us rulers of the earth
Everything under our feet:
All flocks and herds,
The animals of the wild,
Cheetahs, aardvarks, ostriches, bears
Red tailed hawks, eagles, deer
Spiny lobsters, soft shelled crabs,
Great white sharks, king cobras, cod of course
Burmese pythons,
Maine coon cats, meow

Surely these majestic beings were not meant to lie
Beneath our feet,
Surely we can marvel
At the grandeur of creation
Without needing to control the animals

As we control ourselves.

Psalm Nine

1 I will give thanks unto God with my whole heart;
I will show forth all thy marvellous works.
² I will be glad and exult in thee;
I will sing praise to thy name, O thou Most High.
³ When mine enemies turn back,
They stumble and perish at thy presence.
⁴ For thou hast maintained my right and my cause;
Thou sittest in the throne judging righteously.
⁵ Thou hast rebuked the nations, thou hast destroyed the wicked;
Thou hast blotted out their name for ever and ever.
⁶ The enemy are come to an end, they are desolate for ever;
And the cities which thou hast overthrown,
The very remembrance of them is perished.
⁷ But God sitteth as king for ever:
He hath prepared his throne for judgment;
⁸ And he will judge the world in righteousness,
He will minister judgment to the peoples in uprightness.
⁹ God also will be a high tower for the oppressed,
A high tower in times of trouble;
¹⁰ And they that know thy name will put their trust in thee;
For thou, God, hast not forsaken them that seek thee.
¹¹ Sing praises to God, who dwelleth in Zion:
Declare among the people his doings.
¹² For he that maketh inquisition for blood remembereth them;
He forgetteth not the cry of the poor.
¹³ Have mercy upon me, O God;
Behold my affliction which I suffer of them that hate me,
Thou that liftest me up from the gates of death;
¹⁴ That I may show forth all thy praise.
In the gates of the daughter of Zion
I will rejoice in thy salvation.
¹⁵ The nations are sunk down in the pit that they made:
In the net which they hid is their own foot taken.

¹⁶ God hath made himself known, he hath executed judgment:
The wicked is snared in the work of his own hands.
¹⁷ The wicked shall be turned back unto Sheol,
Even all the nations that forget God.
¹⁸ For the needy shall not alway be forgotten,
Nor the expectation of the poor perish for ever.
¹⁹ Arise, O God; let not man prevail:
Let the nations be judged in thy sight.
²⁰ Put them in fear, O God:
Let the nations know themselves to be but men.

Gratitude is all, proclaims the prudent man
The mentally healthy according to form

What fool cannot be grateful for a sunny day?
Make fun if you will of June Moon Spoon
Cuddle up a little closer
In these days of reported provocation and abuse
The Universe delivers still

We sing of wind and rain and even hurricanes
Our enemies stumble
The Nazis and the Japanese destroyed
Only to rise with new generations
Remembering nothing that went before
Not bombs
Not torture
Not prayers of the faithful

On either coast
In the land of former immigrants and savages
There's a church on every corner
Hallelujah and amen
We pray you will bless our survival
Our endurance
Our weaponry
The Lord reigneth forever and ever
So says the Psalm

Get on the right side, Sister

Our courts overflow
With tales of terrorists
And infidels who wish us dead

At the same time
They besiege our gates
Innocent
And eager to arrive

The wicked go down to the realm of the dead,
All the nations that relinquish God

The evangelicals
And the fundamentalists
Insist we will be judged for our iniquity
To be specific:
Homosexuality
Abortions
Lesbians running for office

Embryos are the face of God
The believers say
As they bomb women and children in Iraq
Afghanistan
Somalia
The world in pieces
The mind of man shattered into insanity

God will not forget the needy, says the Psalm
Even as they perish

Strike our enemies with terror, Lord
We praise your contradictions
Your complexity
Your absence
Forever and ever
Amen

Psalm Ten

¹ *Why standest thou afar off, O God?*
Why hidest thou thyself in times of trouble?
² *In the pride of the wicked the poor is hotly pursued;*
Let them be taken in the devices that they have conceived.
³ *For the wicked boasteth of his heart's desire,*
And the covetous renounceth, yea, contemneth God.
⁴ *The wicked, in the pride of his countenance, saith,*
He will not require it.
All his thoughts are, There is no God.
⁵ *His ways are firm at all times;*
Thy judgments are far above out of his sight:
As for all his adversaries, he puffeth at them.
⁶ *He saith in his heart, I shall not be moved;*
To all generations I shall not be in adversity.
⁷ *His mouth is full of cursing and deceit and oppression:*
Under his tongue is mischief and iniquity.
⁸ *He sitteth in the lurking-places of the villages;*
In the secret places doth he murder the innocent;
His eyes are privily set against the helpless.
⁹ *He lurketh in secret as a lion in his covert;*
He lieth in wait to catch the poor:
He doth catch the poor, when he draweth him in his net.
¹⁰ *He croucheth, he boweth down,*
And the helpless fall by his strong ones.
¹¹ *He saith in his heart: God hath forgotten;*
He hideth his face, he will never see it.
¹² *Arise, O God; O God, lift up thy hand:*
Forget not the poor.
¹³ *Wherefore doth the wicked contemn God,*
And say in his heart, Thou wilt not require it?
¹⁴ *Thou hast seen it; for thou beholdest mischief and spite,*
To requite it with thy hand:
The helpless committeth himself unto thee;
Thou hast been the helper of the fatherless.

¹⁵ *Break thou the arm of the wicked;*
And as for the evil man, seek out his wickedness till thou find none.
¹⁶ *God is King for ever and ever:*
The nations are perished out of his land.
¹⁷ *God, thou hast heard the desire of the meek:*
Thou wilt prepare their heart, thou wilt cause thine ear to hear;
¹⁸ *To judge the fatherless and the oppressed,*
That man who is of the earth may be terrible no more.

The prosperity gospel is a billion-dollar industry
God wants us to be rich
Bitch
Jesus died on the cross, didn't he?
The down day of all time

He also rose from the dead
As the story goes
Iridescent
Ready to rule

Conclusion: it's all good news
The law of attraction
Yes Ma'am
I've got resurrection written on my chest

In the meantime
Police shoot black men in the back
His cell phone looked like an Uzi
Said the shooter
Swear to God

The president boasts he's very rich
As the drones of our democracy
Bombard weddings in Afghanistan
Evidently a mistake
Focus on the higher goal
Freedom
And universal suffrage

With God there is success
States the blue-eyed beneficiary of European DNA

The prosperous man announces to himself
"Nothing will ever shake me."
"No one will do me harm"

That way, he lies in wait
And when the moment comes
He does away with gooks
Insurgents raised from birth
To murder us
But no, we have learned to wait, we will,
To drag away the corpses of our enemies
Heads hacked off
Hearts hanging
Memories erased

That's what you do best
You look away
From our sickness and our misery
You look away from famine
And hurricane
You look away
From schizophrenia

Apparently, we're on our own

If we choose to say
Death is your almighty will
Then good
That way
We can play religion too

Arise, Lord! Lift up your heart!
Do not forget us.
You see the trouble of the afflicted
Except you don't

Or if you do
You don't

Sorry about that
I was off my meds
The Lord is King for ever and ever
The nations of his enemies will perish from his land

How's that?

Psalm Eleven

1 In God do I take refuge:
How say ye to my soul,
Flee as a bird to your mountain;
² For, lo, the wicked bend the bow,
They make ready their arrow upon the string,
That they may shoot in darkness at the upright in heart;
³ If the foundations be destroyed,
What can the righteous do?
⁴ God is in his holy temple;
God, his throne is in heaven;
His eyes behold, his eyelids try, the children of men.
⁵ God trieth the righteous;
But the wicked and him that loveth violence his soul hateth.
⁶ Upon the wicked he will rain snares;
Fire and brimstone and burning wind shall be the portion of their cup.
⁷ For God is righteous; he loveth righteousness:
The upright shall behold his face.

I have put my trust in you
Not knowing you
Merely sensing you
Suspecting you

The innate they say
Felt
Not understood
Not tested
No trials
Unsurveyed

Still
For the unknowing

You

Five thousand years of promises
To destroy my enemies
Raining fire and brimstone on whose we call wicked
This, the revealed inheritance
Prayed aloud in the camps
By the evicted and the starved
The butchered
The hanged

As the wicked drove off
Afterwards
To their ceaseless celebrations
In Portofino
Cozumel
And Beverly Hills

Psalm Twelve

1 Help, O God; for the godly man ceaseth;
For the faithful fail from among the children of men.
² They speak falsehood every one with his neighbor:
With flattering lip, and with a double heart, do they speak.
³ God will cut off all flattering lips,
The tongue that speaketh great things;
⁴ Who have said, With our tongue will we prevail;
Our lips are our own: who is lord over us?
⁵ Because of the oppression of the poor,
Because of the sighing of the needy,
Now will I arise, saith God;
I will set him in the safety he panteth for.
⁶ The words of God are pure words;
As silver tried in a furnace on the earth,
Purified seven times.
⁷ Thou wilt keep them, O God,
Thou wilt preserve them from this generation for ever.
⁸ The wicked walk on every side,
When vileness is exalted among the sons of men.

I am surrounded by betrayal
Praised to my face
Flattered loudly
None better, they say

Another version of me
Is visited behind my back
I am misquoted
Defamed
Slandered

Where are you
Who promises to cut off
The lips of my accusers?
Who promises to keep me safe?

You turn me into a corporate wife
To be cheated on relentlessly

You claim
You are truth revealed
When in fact
You are the truth of money
Collected at the door

Psalm Thirteen

1 How long, O God? wilt thou forget me for ever?
How long wilt thou hide thy face from me?
² How long shall I take counsel in my soul,
Having sorrow in my heart all the day?
How long shall mine enemy be exalted over me?
³ Consider and answer me, O God my God:
Lighten mine eyes, lest I sleep the sleep of death;
⁴ Lest mine enemy say, I have prevailed against him;
Lest mine adversaries rejoice when I am moved.
⁵ But I have trusted in thy loving kindness;
My heart shall rejoice in thy salvation.
⁶ I will sing unto God,
Because he hath dealt bountifully with me.

Who will hear me?

Somebody who

Where are you now
Whoever you are?

Lighten my soul
Lift my sorrow

Otherwise
What good
This hunger in my heart?

What sense
Can I ascribe to pain
And loss
Did someone mention death?

They say the world laughs at calamity
The misery of the poor
The sorrows of the elderly

Scratch that
We are here to be entertained
Definitely
The young and the restless
A small screen narrative
Endless coupling
Held together by greasepaint
And subterfuge
Lipstick ruby red
A cacophony of compliments
And lies
The way of the world
A cliché come true.

I remember the simple elements
The beauty of the black brown soil
The laughter of dogs
New life come spring

It's all of a piece
Complexity
Guaranteed

Whoever we are
Remember
We are still the human race.

Kyrie Eleison

Psalm Fourteen

1 The fool hath said in his heart, There is no God.
They are corrupt, they have done abominable works;
There is none that doeth good.
² God looked down from heaven upon the children of men,
To see if there were any that did understand,
That did seek after God.
³ They are all gone aside; they are together become filthy;
There is none that doeth good, no, not one.
⁴ Have all the workers of iniquity no knowledge,
Who eat up my people as they eat bread,
And call not upon God?
⁵ There were they in great fear;
For God is in the generation of the righteous.
⁶ Ye put to shame the counsel of the poor,
Because God is his refuge.
⁷ Oh that the salvation of Israel were come out of Zion!
When God bringeth back the captivity of his people,
Then shall Jacob rejoice, and Israel shall be glad.

The fool hath said in his heart
There is no God
Declares the Psalm, once a simple song
Apparently now absolute
According to Evangelicals

Is the Lord, what a word—
How about potentate?
How about wizir?
Really looking down
Follow the dotted line
To discover men, women, and children
That would be us
Pursuing God?

Is that what He does
Police?
Patrol?
Supervise?

We seek the salvation of Israel
The saying goes
Hoping prophets will return
To reestablish justice
Mercy
And universal love

Did someone say God?

Baby
We can do this ourselves

Can't we?

Oh

Psalm Fifteen

1 God, who shall sojourn in thy tabernacle?
Who shall dwell in thy holy hill?
² He that walketh uprightly, and worketh righteousness,
And speaketh truth in his heart;
³ He that slandereth not with his tongue,
Nor doeth evil to his friend,
Nor taketh up a reproach against his neighbor;
⁴ In whose eyes a reprobate is despised,
But who honoreth them that fear God;
He that sweareth to his own hurt, and changeth not;
⁵ He that putteth not out his money to interest,
Nor taketh reward against the innocent.
He that doeth these things shall never be moved.

Let's hear it
For the righteous
Who tip twenty-five percent
And praise their friends behind their backs
Who never descend into political hysteria
Polarizing, defaming, slandering presidents and vice presidents
All those who have placed their hands on the Bible
Promising to serve the common good

I can think of five
No four
Four just men
Or two?
The Righteous Brothers?
Is that enough?

As for myself
I work on correcting my course
Inevitably off-track
And wandering

One day I will forgive you
For making me mortal
Translated
Deaf
Dumb
And blind
Let's hear it for the righteous
I'm not there yet

Are you?

Psalm Sixteen

1 Preserve me, O God; for in thee do I take refuge.
² O my soul, thou hast said unto God, Thou art my Lord:
I have no good beyond thee.
³ As for the saints that are in the earth,
They are the excellent in whom is all my delight.
⁴ Their sorrows shall be multiplied that give gifts for another god:
Their drink-offerings of blood will I not offer,
Nor take their names upon my lips.
⁵ God is the portion of mine inheritance and of my cup:
Thou maintainest my lot.
⁶ The lines are fallen unto me in pleasant places;
Yea, I have a goodly heritage.
⁷ I will bless God, who hath given me counsel;
Yea, my heart instructeth me in the night seasons.
⁸ I have set God always before me:
Because he is at my right hand, I shall not be moved.
⁹ Therefore my heart is glad, and my glory rejoiceth:
My flesh also shall dwell in safety.
¹⁰ For thou wilt not leave my soul to Sheol;
Neither wilt thou suffer thy holy one to see corruption.
¹¹ Thou wilt show me the path of life:
In thy presence is fulness of joy;
In thy right hand there are pleasures for evermore.

Preserve me
I say to Silence
In Thee I put my trust
Knowing I will be preserved as long as body lasts
And not a second longer
No matter how much I curl up in a ball
Like Sparky
Our yellow Labrador

Hoping no one
Not even you
Will notice me

I am told you will not let my soul remain in hell
Or my flesh corrupt
Although it will surely rot
Ashes to ashes and dust to dust
Who's kidding who?
And whom
And you

In the meantime
I rest in hope
That unlike my dead compatriots
Now cinders in a cookie jar
I will rise into light
Transfigured
And alive

Psalm Seventeen

1 Hear the right, O God, attend unto my cry;
Give ear unto my prayer, that goeth not out of feigned lips.
² Let my sentence come forth from thy presence;
Let thine eyes look upon equity.
³ Thou hast proved my heart; thou hast visited me in the night;
Thou hast tried me, and findest nothing;
I am purposed that my mouth shall not transgress.
⁴ As for the works of men, by the word of thy lips
I have kept me from the ways of the violent.
⁵ My steps have held fast to thy paths,
My feet have not slipped.
⁶ I have called upon thee, for thou wilt answer me, O God:
Incline thine ear unto me, and hear my speech.
⁷ Show thy marvellous loving kindness,
O thou that savest by thy right hand them that take refuge in thee
From those that rise up against them.
⁸ Keep me as the apple of the eye;
Hide me under the shadow of thy wings,
⁹ From the wicked that oppress me,
My deadly enemies, that compass me about.
¹⁰ They are inclosed in their own fat:
With their mouth they speak proudly.
¹¹ They have now compassed us in our steps;
They set their eyes to cast us down to the earth.
¹² He is like a lion that is greedy of his prey,
And as it were a young lion lurking in secret places.
¹³ Arise, O God,
Confront him, cast him down:
Deliver my soul from the wicked by thy sword;
¹⁴ From men by thy hand, O God,
From men of the world, whose portion is in this life,
And whose belly thou fillest with thy treasure:
They are satisfied with children,

And leave the rest of their substance to their babes.
¹⁵ As for me, I shall behold thy face in righteousness;
I shall be satisfied, when I awake, with beholding thy form.

Like everyone else
I pray to be safe
Rich
And to live forever
With all my teeth intact

In the meantime
I am surrounded by lions
And tigers
And Republicans
Who would devour me if they could

Cancer lurks in the shadows
With diabetes close behind
Featuring neuromuscular disease
And lunacy at every turn
Ha ha

Who will stop the lion from ripping my flesh?
Who will protect me from drones
And local alcoholics?

More to the point
Who will save me
From me myself and I?

Is that your purpose –
To make me untouchable
To render me immortal
Unknown
By those around me?

I would surmise
We come here for complicated reasons
None of which I completely understand
My prayer is hear my prayer

When I awaken from this darkness
I hope to see your face
Hear your laughter
And hear you call my name
I need nothing more
Not a house by the waves
Not a Lamborghini
Not even a Performer of the Year award

No, just you

Just you

Psalm Eighteen

1 I love thee, O God, my strength.
2 God is my rock, and my fortress, and my deliverer;
My God, my rock, in whom I will take refuge;
My shield, and the horn of my salvation, my high tower.
3 I will call upon God, who is worthy to be praised:
So shall I be saved from mine enemies.
4 The cords of death compassed me,
And the floods of ungodliness made me afraid.
5 The cords of Sheol were round about me;
The snares of death came upon me.
6 In my distress I called upon God,
And cried unto my God:
He heard my voice out of his temple,
And my cry before him came into his ears.
7 Then the earth shook and trembled;
The foundations also of the mountains quaked
And were shaken, because he was wroth.
8 There went up a smoke out of his nostrils,
And fire out of his mouth devoured:
Coals were kindled by it.
9 He bowed the heavens also, and came down;
And thick darkness was under his feet.
10 And he rode upon a cherub, and did fly;
Yea, he soared upon the wings of the wind.
11 He made darkness his hiding-place, his pavilion round about him,
Darkness of waters, thick clouds of the skies.
12 At the brightness before him his thick clouds passed,
Hailstones and coals of fire.
13 God also thundered in the heavens,
And the Most High uttered his voice,
Hailstones and coals of fire.
14 And he sent out his arrows, and scattered them;
Yea, lightnings manifold, and discomfited them.

¹⁵ Then the channels of waters appeared,
And the foundations of the world were laid bare,
At thy rebuke, O God,
At the blast of the breath of thy nostrils.
¹⁶ He sent from on high, he took me;
He drew me out of many waters.
¹⁷ He delivered me from my strong enemy,
And from them that hated me; for they were too mighty for me.
¹⁸ They came upon me in the day of my calamity;
But God was my stay.
¹⁹ He brought me forth also into a large place;
He delivered me, because he delighted in me.
²⁰ God hath rewarded me according to my righteousness;
According to the cleanness of my hands hath he recompensed me.
²¹ For I have kept the ways of God,
And have not wickedly departed from my God.
²² For all his ordinances were before me,
And I put not away his statutes from me.
²³ I was also perfect with him,
And I kept myself from mine iniquity.
²⁴ Therefore hath God recompensed me according to my righteousness,
According to the cleanness of my hands in his eyesight.
²⁵ With the merciful thou wilt show thyself merciful;
With the perfect man thou wilt show thyself perfect;
²⁶ With the pure thou wilt show thyself pure;
And with the perverse thou wilt show thyself froward.
²⁷ For thou wilt save the afflicted people;
But the haughty eyes thou wilt bring down.
²⁸ For thou wilt light my lamp:
God my God will lighten my darkness.
²⁹ For by thee I run upon a troop;
And by my God do I leap over a wall.
³⁰ As for God, his way is perfect:
The word of God is tried;
He is a shield unto all them that take refuge in him.

³¹ For who is God, save God?
And who is a rock, besides our God,
³² The God that girdeth me with strength,
And maketh my way perfect?
³³ He maketh my feet like hinds' feet:
And setteth me upon my high places.
³⁴ He teacheth my hands to war;
So that mine arms do bend a bow of brass.
³⁵ Thou hast also given me the shield of thy salvation;
And thy right hand hath holden me up,
And thy gentleness hath made me great.
³⁶ Thou hast enlarged my steps under me,
And my feet have not slipped.
³⁷ I will pursue mine enemies, and overtake them;
Neither will I turn again till they are consumed.
³⁸ I will smite them through, so that they shall not be able to rise:
They shall fall under my feet.
³⁹ For thou hast girded me with strength unto the battle:
Thou hast subdued under me those that rose up against me.
⁴⁰ Thou hast also made mine enemies turn their backs unto me,
That I might cut off them that hate me.
⁴¹ They cried, but there was none to save;
Even unto God, but he answered them not.
⁴² Then did I beat them small as the dust before the wind;
I did cast them out as the mire of the streets.
⁴³ Thou hast delivered me from the strivings of the people;
Thou hast made me the head of the nations:
A people whom I have not known shall serve me.
⁴⁴ As soon as they hear of me they shall obey me;
The foreigners shall submit themselves unto me.
⁴⁵ The foreigners shall fade away,
And shall come trembling out of their close places.
⁴⁶ God liveth; and blessed be my rock;
And exalted be the God of my salvation,
⁴⁷ Even the God that executeth vengeance for me,

And subdueth peoples under me.
[48] *He rescueth me from mine enemies;*
Yea, thou liftest me up above them that rise up against me;
Thou deliverest me from the violent man.
[49] *Therefore I will give thanks unto thee, O God, among the nations,*
And will sing praises unto thy name.
[50] *Great deliverance giveth he to his king,*
And showeth loving kindness to his anointed,
To David and to his seed, for evermore.

Someday I will know you
You are my strength
My power
My light
I like to think
Or at least to imagine

In the meantime
You are only sensed
As if you hide beyond a row of hills
We call you our Rock
Our Might
Our Deliverer

By the way
Where were you at Gettysburg?
Shiloh
Fort Donelson
Chattanooga
Antietam
Yellow Tavern
Nashville
Mobile Bay
Five Forks
Gettysburg
Always that

Before the beginning
Of who we became
The Battle of Camden
Barefoot soldiers eating grass
In the glaring Carolina sun

The sorrows of death encompassed us
And pressed us down
We called upon your holy name
As boys surrendered to the dirt
Their brains blown to smithereens
Innards splattered
Dreaming dashed

Did you hurl the lightning?
Did you send the storm?

We said you saved us
Even as the majority went down.

Will you show yourself to be merciful?
We are a nation destroyed
A people in anguish
We stand convinced you will rescue us
As we lay slain and torn apart
We still believe in you
We have nothing else
Only ourselves
And we are beaten down

You breathed into us
Weapons of steel
And domination
You offered dreams of victory
Of the world we left behind
Of slaves for the taking
According to your holy laws

To please you we pursued our enemies
To please you we became invincible
Until we were dust under the feet
Of those who destroyed us

We prayed to you
To deliver us
From our enemies

Now the war is lost
The fields are burned and barren
We are reviled
And ridiculed

Still
We persist in giving thanks unto thee

And why is that?

Psalm Nineteen

1 The heavens declare the glory of God;
And the firmament showeth his handiwork.
² Day unto day uttereth speech,
And night unto night showeth knowledge.
³ There is no speech nor language;
Their voice is not heard.
⁴ Their line is gone out through all the earth,
And their words to the end of the world.
In them hath he set a tabernacle for the sun,
⁵ Which is as a bridegroom coming out of his chamber,
And rejoiceth as a strong man to run his course.
⁶ His going forth is from the end of the heavens,
And his circuit unto the ends of it;
And there is nothing hid from the heat thereof.
⁷ The law of God is perfect, restoring the soul:
The testimony of God is sure, making wise the simple.
⁸ The precepts of God are right, rejoicing the heart:
The commandment of God is pure, enlightening the eyes.
⁹ The fear of God is clean, enduring for ever:
The ordinances of God are true, and righteous altogether.
¹⁰ More to be desired are they than gold, yea, than much fine gold;
Sweeter also than honey and the droppings of the honeycomb.
¹¹ Moreover by them is thy servant warned:
In keeping them there is great reward.
¹² Who can discern his errors?
Clear thou me from hidden faults.
¹³ Keep back thy servant also from presumptuous sins;
Let them not have dominion over me:
Then shall I be upright,
And I shall be clear from great transgression.
¹⁴ Let the words of my mouth and the meditation of my heart
Be acceptable in thy sight,
O God, my rock, and my redeemer.

The heavens parade a billion stars
Beauty where no one breathes

The earth cries complexity
At times glorious
Too often terrible

In April
Carolina comes alive
Silently, the deer appear
Watching us
Through the blush of azaleas and ornamental pear

Believers rejoice in the testimony of the Lord
His commandment is pure enough they say
His authority is paramount

As we look on
Waiting for opportunities
And rescuers

We are righteous in our truths
Forgoing fantasy
Sloughing off directives
From those who would buy and sell
Our blood and brains

Who will protect us?
Who will redeem us?
Who will hear?

Let the words of our mouths be acceptable
In the sight of our rescuers

Whoever you are

Psalm Twenty

1 God answer thee in the day of trouble;
The name of the God of Jacob set thee up on high;
² Send thee help from the sanctuary,
And strengthen thee out of Zion;
³ Remember all thy offerings,
And accept thy burnt-sacrifice;
⁴ Grant thee thy heart's desire,
And fulfil all thy counsel.
⁵ We will triumph in thy salvation,
And in the name of our God we will set up our banners:
God fulfil all thy petitions.
⁶ Now know I that God saveth his anointed;
He will answer him from his holy heaven
With the saving strength of his right hand.
⁷ Some trust in chariots, and some in horses;
But we will make mention of the name of God our God.
⁸ They are bowed down and fallen;
But we are risen, and stand upright.
⁹ Save, God:
Let the King answer us when we call.

Will troubles come again?
Will cannons boom in the capitals
Return us to misery
And destroy the families
We have come to love?

Our prayers rise to heaven
With the cries of the wounded
Evaporating in the upper air

The North invades
What more to say?

We are not rescued
And no longer honored
No longer anointed

We cry out and no one hears
We lament and no one mourns
We are fallen

Who will hear us?
Who will rescue us?

Psalm Twenty-one

1 The king shall joy in thy strength, O God;
And in thy salvation how greatly shall he rejoice!
² Thou hast given him his heart's desire,
And hast not withholden the request of his lips.
³ For thou meetest him with the blessings of goodness:
Thou settest a crown of fine gold on his head.
⁴ He asked life of thee, thou gavest it him,
Even length of days for ever and ever.
⁵ His glory is great in thy salvation:
Honor and majesty dost thou lay upon him.
⁶ For thou makest him most blessed for ever:
Thou makest him glad with joy in thy presence.
⁷ For the king trusteth in God;
And through the loving kindness of the Most High
He shall not be moved.
⁸ Thy hand will find out all thine enemies;
Thy right hand will find out those that hate thee.
⁹ Thou wilt make them as a fiery furnace in the time of thine anger:
God will swallow them up in his wrath,
And the fire shall devour them.
¹⁰ Their fruit wilt thou destroy from the earth,
And their seed from among the children of men.
¹¹ For they intended evil against thee;
They conceived a device which they are not able to perform.
¹² For thou wilt make them turn their back;
Thou wilt make ready with thy bowstrings against their face.
¹³ Be thou exalted, O God, in thy strength:
So will we sing and praise thy power.

God is on our side
No doubt

Our government is crowned with gold
Literal and metaphorical
Our ruling class gives thanks to God

The rest of us are schooled
To thank the King
Leader by Divine Right
O Lord
You have placed him there

The will of the people
Want him to regulate
With an iron fist
So they can be safe from interlopers
And foreigners
From slaves and former slaves
Looking for revenge

We will root out your enemies
We will burn them
We will destroy their posterity

They shall be devoured
Their history destroyed
Their languages erased
Their music ridiculed

In your Holy Name

Amen

Psalm Twenty-two

1 My God, my God, why hast thou forsaken me?
Why art thou so far from helping me,
And from the words of my groaning?
² O my God, I cry in the daytime, but thou answerest not;
And in the night season, and am not silent.
³ But thou art holy,
O thou that inhabitest the praises of Israel.
⁴ Our fathers trusted in thee:
They trusted, and thou didst deliver them.
⁵ They cried unto thee, and were delivered:
They trusted in thee, and were not put to shame.
⁶ But I am a worm, and no man;
A reproach of men, and despised of the people.
⁷ All they that see me laugh me to scorn:
They shoot out the lip, they shake the head, saying,
⁸ Commit thyself unto God; let him deliver him:
Let him rescue him, seeing he delighteth in him.
⁹ But thou art he that took me out of the womb;
Thou didst make me trust when I was upon my mother's breasts.
¹⁰ I was cast upon thee from the womb;
Thou art my God since my mother bare me.
¹¹ Be not far from me; for trouble is near;
For there is none to help.
¹² Many bulls have compassed me;
Strong bulls of Bashan have beset me round.
¹³ They gape upon me with their mouth,
As a ravening and a roaring lion.
¹⁴ I am poured out like water,
And all my bones are out of joint:
My heart is like wax;
It is melted within me.
¹⁵ My strength is dried up like a potsherd;
And my tongue cleaveth to my jaws;

And thou hast brought me into the dust of death.
¹⁶ For dogs have compassed me:
A company of evil-doers have inclosed me;
They pierced my hands and my feet.
¹⁷ I may count all my bones.
They look and stare upon me;
¹⁸ They part my garments among them,
And upon my vesture do they cast lots.
¹⁹ But be not thou far off, O God:
O thou my succor, haste thee to help me.
²⁰ Deliver my soul from the sword,
My darling from the power of the dog.
²¹ Save me from the lion's mouth;
Yea, from the horns of the wild-oxen thou hast answered me.
²² I will declare thy name unto my brethren:
In the midst of the assembly will I praise thee.
²³ Ye that fear God, praise him;
All ye the seed of Jacob, glorify him;
And stand in awe of him, all ye the seed of Israel.
²⁴ For he hath not despised nor abhorred the affliction of the afflicted;
Neither hath he hid his face from him;
But when he cried unto him, he heard.
²⁵ Of thee cometh my praise in the great assembly:
I will pay my vows before them that fear him.
²⁶ The meek shall eat and be satisfied;
They shall praise God that seek after him:
Let your heart live for ever.
²⁷ All the ends of the earth shall remember and turn unto God;
And all the kindreds of the nations shall worship before thee.
²⁸ For the kingdom is God's;
And he is the ruler over the nations.
²⁹ All the fat ones of the earth shall eat and worship:
All they that go down to the dust shall bow before him,
Even he that cannot keep his soul alive.
³⁰ A seed shall serve him;
It shall be told of the Lord unto the next generation.

³¹ *They shall come and shall declare his righteousness*
Unto a people that shall be born, that he hath done it.

My God, my God, why hast thou forsaken me?
Said the Son of Man

The rest of us—
Who hears our roar?
The historians?

Who is this divinity we talk about
And sometimes remember to address?

Our parents trusted you
And said simply
You answer prayers

Jesus said if we ask for an egg
Will you give us a stone?

    Ask and it shall be given to you

Grandma asked for money
And it always came, she said

So far so good

We are the new generation
Subsisting on opioids
Anti-depressants
Oxycontin
Fentanyl
Heroin
Haagen Dazs
Salted caramel
Who cares about calories?

My six-hundred-pound life
The Center of the Universe

I wait upon the so-called lord
Drowning in despair

Deliver my soul.
None but you
Can keep it alive
None but you
Can hear my cry

In the meantime
Please pass the Krispy Kremes

Psalm Twenty–three

1 The LORD is my shepherd; I shall not want.
² He maketh me to lie down in green pastures;
He leadeth me beside still waters.
³ He restoreth my soul:
He guideth me in the paths of righteousness for his name's sake.
⁴ Yea, though I walk through the valley of the shadow of death,
I will fear no evil; for thou art with me;
Thy rod and thy staff, they comfort me.
⁵ Thou preparest a table before me in the presence of mine enemies:
Thou hast anointed my head with oil;
My cup runneth over.
⁶ Surely goodness and loving kindness shall follow me
All the days of my life;
And I shall dwell in the house of God for ever.

The Lord is my shepherd; I shall not want
Said the debutante
With the Alpha Romeo and the Charleston pedigree

He maketh me lie down in green pastures
She continued on
Thinking of the first time she gave it away
Except she never gave nothin' away
She always had a price
Lying in a wildflowered field once devoted to Irish potatoes
In Bridgehampton near the beach
And the relentless summer sun

For ten minutes she restored her soul
And forgot about wild dogs and copperheads
And the man who fucked her
And forgot how to pray
She said

Except she didn't forget
She never did

She knew the beauty of the surrounding world
And the kindness of the friends who rescued her
And she was whole again

In spite of ritual
Diamonds are forever
Emeralds too
That and never-ending pedigree

And pearls

What time does the party start?

Psalm Twenty-four

1 The earth is God's, and the fulness thereof;
The world, and they that dwell therein.
² For he hath founded it upon the seas,
And established it upon the floods.
³ Who shall ascend into the hill of God?
And who shall stand in his holy place?
⁴ He that hath clean hands, and a pure heart;
Who hath not lifted up his soul unto falsehood,
And hath not sworn deceitfully.
⁵ He shall receive a blessing from God,
And righteousness from the God of his salvation.
⁶ This is the generation of them that seek after him,
That seek thy face, even Jacob.
⁷ Lift up your heads, O ye gates;
And be ye lifted up, ye everlasting doors:
And the King of glory will come in.
⁸ Who is the King of glory?
God strong and mighty,
God mighty in battle.
⁹ Lift up your heads, O ye gates;
Yea, lift them up, ye everlasting doors:
And the King of glory will come in.
¹⁰ Who is this King of glory?
God of hosts,
He is the King of glory.

The earth we once called Gaia
A goddess who sustained humanity
That would be us
Wraps herself in the oceans
And the wilderness

She breathes beauty
Calls forth birdsong
And embraces all living things

Who dares pollute her body
Ravage her beauty
Defile her heart
And scar her eternal face?

She provides a place for us
Unto the millennia
She blesses us
With breeze and crystal waters
And blossoming trees
That give us everything we need to thrive

Who is this Gaia
This mother of all
This presence among us?
How do we thank her?
How do we respond in grace?

Psalm Twenty-five

1 Unto thee, O God, do I lift up my soul.
² O my God, in thee have I trusted,
Let me not be put to shame;
Let not mine enemies triumph over me.
³ Yea, none that wait for thee shall be put to shame:
They shall be put to shame that deal treacherously without cause.
⁴ Show me thy ways, O God;
Teach me thy paths.
⁵ Guide me in thy truth, and teach me;
For thou art the God of my salvation;
For thee do I wait all the day.
⁶ Remember, O God, thy tender mercies and thy loving kindness;
For they have been ever of old.
⁷ Remember not the sins of my youth, nor my transgressions:
According to thy loving kindness remember thou me,
For thy goodness' sake, O God.
⁸ Good and upright is God:
Therefore will he instruct sinners in the way.
⁹ The meek will he guide in justice;
And the meek will he teach his way.
¹⁰ All the paths of God are loving kindness and truth
Unto such as keep his covenant and his testimonies.
¹¹ For thy name's sake, O God,
Pardon mine iniquity, for it is great.
¹² What man is he that feareth God?
Him shall he instruct in the way that he shall choose.
¹³ His soul shall dwell at ease;
And his seed shall inherit the land.
¹⁴ The friendship of God is with them that fear him;
And he will show them his covenant.
¹⁵ Mine eyes are ever toward God;
For he will pluck my feet out of the net.
¹⁶ Turn thee unto me, and have mercy upon me;

For I am desolate and afflicted.
¹⁷ The troubles of my heart are enlarged:
Oh bring thou me out of my distresses.
¹⁸ Consider mine affliction and my travail;
And forgive all my sins.
¹⁹ Consider mine enemies, for they are many;
And they hate me with cruel hatred.
²⁰ Oh keep my soul, and deliver me:
Let me not be put to shame, for I take refuge in thee.
²¹ Let integrity and uprightness preserve me,
For I wait for thee.
²² Redeem Israel, O God,
Out of all his troubles.

I pray to the Lord to lift my soul
But first
Let me hunt down terrorists
I know they're there
With scarves around their faces
Bombs in their backpacks
And languages that make no sense
Except to them

I pray that former slaves
And heretics
Unhappy as hell
Move back to where they came from
And leave us alone
To own the earth
And possibly the sky

Show me the way, O Lord.
Teach me to be cunning
Like feral cats
And cottonmouths

Save me
From drinking too much
Driving too fast
Using too many drugs
And four-letter words

Lead me in truth, O Lord
And I will destroy your enemies
Bombs over Tokyo
Hurray

Good and upright is the Lord
He will teach the radicals
The way, the light and the truth
Or fair warning
they will be extinguished on the spot

The meek will he guide in judgment
The submissive will he teach his way
That would be us
Blind obedience

Our souls shall dwell at ease
Our seed shall inherit the earth
Yes, Ma'am

Psalm Twenty-six

1 Judge me, O God, for I have walked in mine integrity:
I have trusted also in God without wavering.
² Examine me, O God, and prove me;
Try my heart and my mind.
³ For thy loving kindness is before mine eyes;
And I have walked in thy truth.
⁴ I have not sat with men of falsehood;
Neither will I go in with dissemblers.
⁵ I hate the assembly of evil-doers,
And will not sit with the wicked.
⁶ I will wash my hands in innocency:
So will I compass thine altar, O God;
⁷ That I may make the voice of thanksgiving to be heard,
And tell of all thy wondrous works.
⁸ God, I love the habitation of thy house,
And the place where thy glory dwelleth.
⁹ Gather not my soul with sinners,
Nor my life with men of blood;
¹⁰ In whose hands is wickedness,
And their right hand is full of bribes.
¹¹ But as for me, I will walk in mine integrity:
Redeem me, and be merciful unto me.
¹² My foot standeth in an even place:
In the congregations will I bless God.

Who judges me?
By whose standards?
Based on what?

I seem attracted to fools
And dissemblers
Otherwise known as phony baloneys
Is that because I'm bored
Or need to feel superior?

Why do I not concentrate
On light instead
And beautiful women
Both on and off screen

What about classical jazz?

Do I know what I'm talking about?

And politicians
Who are honest and sincere
A contradiction in terms

Putting myself aside
If that's possible
I'm glad to be here
Present and accounted for
Waiting on someone
To rescue me

Maybe even from myself

My hope is in the Lord

Psalm Twenty-seven

1 God is my light and my salvation;
Whom shall I fear?
God is the strength of my life;
Of whom shall I be afraid?
² When evil-doers came upon me to eat up my flesh,
Even mine adversaries and my foes, they stumbled and fell.
³ Though a host should encamp against me,
My heart shall not fear:
Though war should rise against me,
Even then will I be confident.
⁴ One thing have I asked of God, that will I seek after:
That I may dwell in the house of God all the days of my life,
To behold the beauty of God,
And to inquire in his temple.
⁵ For in the day of trouble he will keep me secretly in his pavilion:
In the covert of his tabernacle will he hide me;
He will lift me up upon a rock.
⁶ And now shall my head be lifted up above mine enemies
Round about me;
And I will offer in his tabernacle sacrifices of joy;
I will sing, yea, I will sing praises unto God.
⁷ Hear, O God, when I cry with my voice:
Have mercy also upon me, and answer me.
⁸ When thou saidst, Seek ye my face; my heart said unto thee,
Thy face, God, will I seek.
⁹ Hide not thy face from me;
Put not thy servant away in anger:
Thou hast been my help;
Cast me not off, neither forsake me, O God of my salvation.
¹⁰ When my father and my mother forsake me,
Then God will take me up.
¹¹ Teach me thy way, O God;

And lead me in a plain path,
Because of mine enemies.
¹² *Deliver me not over unto the will of mine adversaries:*
For false witnesses are risen up against me,
And such as breathe out cruelty.
¹³ *I had fainted, unless I had believed to see the goodness of God*
In the land of the living.
¹⁴ *Wait for God:*
Be strong, and let thy heart take courage;
Yea, wait thou for God.

Something
Beyond myself
Beyond my comprehension
Beyond knowing
And sensing
And argument
Gives me strength

When I stop wondering about how weak I am
And put off food and alcohol and drugs
And my addiction to everything alive
But me

When I surrender to that something
That imperceptible night
I am suddenly filled with light
A light known only to me

Where are you now?
Hear me
Show me your face

When I am rejected
And pushed away
And refused
All manner of love and legacy

Show me the path
Show me your heart
Give me the courage

To wait

Psalm Twenty-eight

1 Unto thee, O God, will I call:
My rock, be not thou deaf unto me;
Lest, if thou be silent unto me,
I become like them that go down into the pit.
² Hear the voice of my supplications, when I cry unto thee,
When I lift up my hands toward thy holy oracle.
³ Draw me not away with the wicked,
And with the workers of iniquity;
That speak peace with their neighbors,
But mischief is in their hearts.
⁴ Give them according to their work,
And according to the wickedness of their doings:
Give them after the operation of their hands;
Render to them their desert.
⁵ Because they regard not the works of God,
Nor the operation of his hands,
He will break them down and not build them up.
⁶ Blessed be God,
Because he hath heard the voice of my supplications.
⁷ God is my strength and my shield;
My heart hath trusted in him, and I am helped:
Therefore my heart greatly rejoiceth;
And with my song will I praise him.
⁸ God is their strength,
And he is a stronghold of salvation to his anointed.
⁹ Save thy people, and bless thine inheritance:
Be their shepherd also, and bear them up for ever.

I cry and no one hears
You stay silent
While I go down into the pit
Why do you punish me?
Why are you invisible?

Yes, we were the wicked ones
Bringing slaves
By the millions
To be beaten down
Drowned
Hanged
And otherwise erased

We first destroyed the people living here

Is that why you are silent?

In your name
You promised us
You would smite our enemies
Destroy the infidels
As we gave glory to your name.

I lift my voice to you
Hear me
Blessed be you
Love me
We are your anointed
Look at us
We are your inheritance

Psalm Twenty-nine

1 *Ascribe unto God, O ye sons of the mighty,*
Ascribe unto God glory and strength.
² *Ascribe unto God the glory due unto his name;*
Worship God in holy array.
³ *The voice of God is upon the waters:*
The God of glory thundereth,
Even God upon many waters.
⁴ *The voice of God is powerful;*
The voice of God is full of majesty.
⁵ *The voice of God breaketh the cedars;*
Yea, God breaketh in pieces the cedars of Lebanon.
⁶ *He maketh them also to skip like a calf;*
Lebanon and Sirion like a young wild-ox.
⁷ *The voice of God cleaveth the flames of fire.*
⁸ *The voice of God shaketh the wilderness;*
God shaketh the wilderness of Kadesh.
⁹ *The voice of God maketh the hinds to calve,*
And strippeth the forests bare:
And in his temple everything saith, Glory.
¹⁰ *God sat as King at the Flood;*
Yea, God sitteth as King for ever.
¹¹ *God will give strength unto his people;*
God will bless his people with peace.

W ho is to be given glory?
Would that be God?
Is that why we are here?
To crawl before a deity?

Is that why we created an anthropomorphic, humanistic God
Who apparently sits on his heavenly throne
Expecting the human race
To proclaim his name?
Is that it?

We fixate on the name of God
Lord Imperator Governor General King
Pick your pedigree
The maker of majesty
Shaking the wilderness
Blazing forth like the eternal sun
Which incidentally will be extinguished
In more or less a billion years
Give or take

This is God?

Bless your people with peace, we pray
Can we not bless ourselves?

Can we not come to terms with who we are?

What are we waiting for?

Psalm Thirty

1 I will extol thee, O God; for thou hast raised me up,
And hast not made my foes to rejoice over me.
² O God my God,
I cried unto thee, and thou hast healed me.
³ O God, thou hast brought up my soul from Sheol;
Thou hast kept me alive, that I should not go down to the pit.
⁴ Sing praise unto God, O ye saints of his,
And give thanks to his holy memorial name.
⁵ For his anger is but for a moment;
His favor is for a life-time:
Weeping may tarry for the night,
But joy cometh in the morning.
⁶ As for me, I said in my prosperity,
I shall never be moved.
⁷ Thou, God, of thy favor hadst made my mountain to stand strong:
Thou didst hide thy face; I was troubled.
⁸ I cried to thee, O God;
And unto God I made supplication:
⁹ What profit is there in my blood, when I go down to the pit?
Shall the dust praise thee? shall it declare thy truth?
¹⁰ Hear, O God, and have mercy upon me:
God, be thou my helper.
¹¹ Thou hast turned for me my mourning into dancing;
Thou hast loosed my sackcloth, and girded me with gladness;
¹² To the end that my glory may sing praise to thee, and not be silent.
O God my God, I will give thanks unto thee for ever.

How have I lasted this long?
And come back from the dead
A hundred times
From illness and insult
And the ruination
Of all I pretended to be?

Is it you?
Have you healed me?
Have you kept me alive?

Despite myself
I am made to sing your name
And cry out to you
Fool that I am

When no one answers me
When the world turns upside down
When I am locked in a pit of despair
I am advised
It is your holy will
Making me think
The only god is
Insanity

O my God
I give thanks unto thee for ever and ever

Why?

Psalm Thirty-one

1 In thee, O God, do I take refuge;
Let me never be put to shame:
Deliver me in thy righteousness.
² Bow down thine ear unto me; deliver me speedily:
Be thou to me a strong rock,
A house of defence to save me.
³ For thou art my rock and my fortress;
Therefore for thy name's sake lead me and guide me.
⁴ Pluck me out of the net that they have laid privily for me;
For thou art my stronghold.
⁵ Into thy hand I commend my spirit:
Thou hast redeemed me, O God, thou God of truth.
⁶ I hate them that regard lying vanities;
But I trust in God.
⁷ I will be glad and rejoice in thy loving kindness;
For thou hast seen my affliction:
Thou hast known my soul in adversities;
⁸ And thou hast not shut me up into the hand of the enemy;
Thou hast set my feet in a large place.
⁹ Have mercy upon me, O God, for I am in distress:
Mine eye wasteth away with grief, yea, my soul and my body.
¹⁰ For my life is spent with sorrow,
And my years with sighing:
My strength faileth because of mine iniquity,
And my bones are wasted away.
¹¹ Because of all mine adversaries I am become a reproach,
Yea, unto my neighbors exceedingly,
And a fear to mine acquaintance:
They that did see me without fled from me.
¹² I am forgotten as a dead man out of mind:
I am like a broken vessel.

¹³ *For I have heard the defaming of many,*
Terror on every side:
While they took counsel together against me,
They devised to take away my life.
¹⁴ *But I trusted in thee, O God:*
I said, Thou art my God.
¹⁵ *My times are in thy hand:*
Deliver me from the hand of mine enemies,
And from them that persecute me.
¹⁶ *Make thy face to shine upon thy servant:*
Save me in thy loving kindness.
¹⁷ *Let me not be put to shame, O God; for I have called upon thee:*
Let the wicked be put to shame, let them be silent in Sheol.
¹⁸ *Let the lying lips be dumb,*
Which speak against the righteous insolently,
With pride and contempt.
¹⁹ *Oh how great is thy goodness,*
Which thou hast laid up for them that fear thee,
Which thou hast wrought for them that take refuge in thee,
Before the sons of men!
²⁰ *In the covert of thy presence wilt thou hide them*
From the plottings of man:
Thou wilt keep them secretly in a pavilion from the strife of tongues.
²¹ *Blessed be God;*
For he hath showed me his marvellous loving kindness in a strong city.
²² *As for me, I said in my haste,*
I am cut off from before thine eyes:
Nevertheless thou heardest the voice of my supplications,
When I cried unto thee.
²³ *Oh love God, all ye his saints:*
God preserveth the faithful,
And plentifully rewardeth him that dealeth proudly.
²⁴ *Be strong, and let your heart take courage,*
All ye that hope in God.

I put my trust in what I've been told
My rock and my fortress
Lead me
Guide me
Is that how it goes?

    Into thy hands I commend my spirit

Does that mean I'm dead and gone?

We will blow up the earth
If we have to
To protect us from our enemies
We're done it before
We'll do it again
Thas right

We've prayed to you a million times
A crapshoot
No, a lottery
Written in the wind they say
Most likely in the ocean too

You know when every sparrow falls
You say
We are falling
Falling into oblivion
And where are you?

Where are you going
And where have you been?

Have mercy on me.
Have mercy on the lot of us

Be of good courage
He shall strengthen your heart
All ye that hope in the Lord

And so it goes

Psalm Thirty-two

1 Blessed is he whose transgression is forgiven,
Whose sin is covered.
² Blessed is the man unto whom God imputeth not iniquity,
And in whose spirit there is no guile.
³ When I kept silence, my bones wasted away
Through my groaning all the day long.
⁴ For day and night thy hand was heavy upon me:
My moisture was changed as with the drought of summer.
⁵ I acknowledged my sin unto thee,
And mine iniquity did I not hide:
I said, I will confess my transgressions unto God;
And thou forgavest the iniquity of my sin.
⁶ For this let every one that is godly pray unto thee in a time
When thou mayest be found:
Surely when the great waters overflow they shall not reach unto him.
⁷ Thou art my hiding-place; thou wilt preserve me from trouble;
Thou wilt compass me about with songs of deliverance.
⁸ I will instruct thee and teach thee in the way which thou shalt go:
I will counsel thee with mine eye upon thee.
⁹ Be ye not as the horse, or as the mule, which have no understanding;
Whose trappings must be bit and bridle to hold them in,
Else they will not come near unto thee.
¹⁰ Many sorrows shall be to the wicked;
But he that trusteth in God, loving kindness shall compass him about.
¹¹ Be glad in God, and rejoice, ye righteous;
And shout for joy, all ye that are upright in heart.

What sins must I confess
To whom must I confess them?

"Excuse me for being alive?"
Is that it?

Am I taking up too much space?
Breathing too much air?
The Bible talks of transgressions
And iniquities
What does that mean?

What happened to us
Since we were innocent?

Lies and fraud
And warmongering maybe
Saber rattling
And sometimes dropping bombs?
Where did we learn that?

I remain a simple bourgeoisie
Unfamiliar to the world
And future history
Almost invisible
An echo of the wind

Be glad in the Lord, and rejoice, ye righteous
And shout for joy
All ye that are upright in heart

For once
Forget your sins
Forget yourself
Open your heart
And love

That's what it says
That's what it says

Psalm Thirty-three

1 Rejoice in God, O ye righteous:
Praise is comely for the upright.
² Give thanks unto God with the harp:
Sing praises unto him with the psaltery of ten strings.
³ Sing unto him a new song;
Play skilfully with a loud noise.
⁴ For the word of God is right;
And all his work is done in faithfulness.
⁵ He loveth righteousness and justice:
The earth is full of the loving kindness of God.
⁶ By the word of God were the heavens made,
And all the host of them by the breath of his mouth.
⁷ He gathereth the waters of the sea together as a heap:
He layeth up the deeps in store-houses.
⁸ Let all the earth fear God:
Let all the inhabitants of the world stand in awe of him.
⁹ For he spake, and it was done;
He commanded, and it stood fast.
¹⁰ God bringeth the counsel of the nations to nought;
He maketh the thoughts of the peoples to be of no effect.
¹¹ The counsel of God standeth fast for ever,
The thoughts of his heart to all generations.
¹² Blessed is the nation whose God is God,
The people whom he hath chosen for his own inheritance.
¹³ God looketh from heaven;
He beholdeth all the sons of men;
¹⁴ From the place of his habitation he looketh forth
Upon all the inhabitants of the earth,
¹⁵ He that fashioneth the hearts of them all,
That considereth all their works.
¹⁶ There is no king saved by the multitude of a host:
A mighty man is not delivered by great strength.
¹⁷ A horse is a vain thing for safety;

Neither doth he deliver any by his great power.
[18] Behold, the eye of God is upon them that fear him,
Upon them that hope in his loving kindness;
[19] To deliver their soul from death,
And to keep them alive in famine.
[20] Our soul hath waited for God:
He is our help and our shield.
[21] For our heart shall rejoice in him,
Because we have trusted in his holy name.
[22] Let thy loving kindness, O God, be upon us,
According as we have hoped in thee.

How many more thousand years
Will it take
For this human tribe
We glorious barbarians
Blood on our faces
Tribal to the point of genocide
To come to terms with this so-called Lord?

This God we sing about
And praise his Holy Name
In our infinite wisdom
As we smash our enemies
Advancing past swords
And guillotines
To drones and depleted uranium

In the name of freedom and democracy
All things bright and beautiful
By the word of the Lord were the heavens made
We pray
We say

Blessed be the people
He hath chosen for his inheritance
We assume those people would be us
He will deliver our souls from death we say

He will keep us alive in famine
And pestilence
Is that so?

What about delirium tremens
Schizophrenia
Alzheimers
And everything else that
Makes you wonder
Why we're here
Let thy mercy, O Lord, be upon us
According as we hope in thee

Psalm Thirty-four

1 I will bless God at all times:
His praise shall continually be in my mouth.
² My soul shall make her boast in God:
The meek shall hear thereof, and be glad.
³ Oh magnify God with me,
And let us exalt his name together.
⁴ I sought God, and he answered me,
And delivered me from all my fears.
⁵ They looked unto him, and were radiant;
And their faces shall never be confounded.
⁶ This poor man cried, and God heard him,
And saved him out of all his troubles.
⁷ The angel of God encampeth round about them that fear him,
And delivereth them.
⁸ Oh taste and see that God is good:
Blessed is the man that taketh refuge in him.
⁹ Oh fear God, ye his saints;
For there is no want to them that fear him.
¹⁰ The young lions do lack, and suffer hunger;
But they that seek God shall not want any good thing.
¹¹ Come, ye children, hearken unto me:
I will teach you the fear of God.
¹² What man is he that desireth life,
And loveth many days, that he may see good?
¹³ Keep thy tongue from evil,
And thy lips from speaking guile.
¹⁴ Depart from evil, and do good;
Seek peace, and pursue it.
¹⁵ The eyes of God are toward the righteous,
And his ears are open unto their cry.
¹⁶ The face of God is against them that do evil,
To cut off the remembrance of them from the earth.
¹⁷ The righteous cried, and God heard,

And delivered them out of all their troubles.
[18] God is nigh unto them that are of a broken heart,
And saveth such as are of a contrite spirit.
[19] Many are the afflictions of the righteous;
But God delivereth him out of them all.
[20] He keepeth all his bones:
Not one of them is broken.
[21] Evil shall slay the wicked;
And they that hate the righteous shall be condemned.
[22] God redeemeth the soul of his servants;
And none of them that take refuge in him shall be condemned.

Put aside the Lord
Praise the human race
For our courage to continue on
In the face of Holocaust and genocide
And lies

Praise inventors
And scientists
Painters
Dancers, actors, poets
Psychiatrists and oncologists
And especially trauma therapists

Yes, praise the clergy more or less
Praise all those who choose the holy spirit
Of the evolving heart

Put aside your waiting on the Lord
Look to yourselves
And your powers of design

Praise fishermen
And farmers

Look for those displaced
And beaten down
Disrespected
By those whose only truth
Is coin

Put aside graven images
Of gods who never were
Except in the imagination of
Executioners and kings

In the meantime
Do good
Keep oceans clean
Let children laugh
And lovers lie together in the sun
Bind up the wounds of the broken down
And the desolate

And in your mercy
You will find your souls

Psalm Thirty-five

1 Strive thou, O God, with them that strive with me:
Fight thou against them that fight against me.
² Take hold of shield and buckler,
And stand up for my help.
³ Draw out also the spear, and stop the way
Against them that pursue me:
Say unto my soul, I am thy salvation.
⁴ Let them be put to shame and brought to dishonor
That seek after my soul:
Let them be turned back and confounded that devise my hurt.
⁵ Let them be as chaff before the wind,
And the angel of God driving them on.
⁶ Let their way be dark and slippery,
And the angel of God pursuing them.
⁷ For without cause have they hid for me their net in a pit;
Without cause have they digged a pit for my soul.
⁸ Let destruction come upon him unawares;
And let his net that he hath hid catch himself:
With destruction let him fall therein.
⁹ And my soul shall be joyful in God:
It shall rejoice in his salvation.
¹⁰ All my bones shall say, God, who is like unto thee,
Who deliverest the poor from him that is too strong for him,
Yea, the poor and the needy from him that robbeth him?
¹¹ Unrighteous witnesses rise up;
They ask me of things that I know not.
¹² They reward me evil for good,
To the bereaving of my soul.
¹³ But as for me, when they were sick, my clothing was sackcloth:
I afflicted my soul with fasting;
And my prayer returned into mine own bosom.
¹⁴ I behaved myself as though it had been my friend or my brother:
I bowed down mourning, as one that bewaileth his mother.

¹⁵ *But in mine adversity they rejoiced,*
And gathered themselves together:
The abjects gathered themselves together against me, and I knew it not;
They did tear me, and ceased not:
¹⁶ *Like the profane mockers in feasts,*
They gnashed upon me with their teeth.
¹⁷ *Lord, how long wilt thou look on?*
Rescue my soul from their destructions,
My darling from the lions.
¹⁸ *I will give thee thanks in the great assembly:*
I will praise thee among much people.
¹⁹ *Let not them that are mine enemies wrongfully rejoice over me;*
Neither let them wink with the eye that hate me without a cause.
²⁰ *For they speak not peace;*
But they devise deceitful words against them that are quiet in the land.
²¹ *Yea, they opened their mouth wide against me;*
They said, Aha, aha, our eye hath seen it.
²² *Thou hast seen it, O God; keep not silence:*
O Lord, be not far from me.
²³ *Stir up thyself, and awake to the justice due unto me,*
Even unto my cause, my God and my Lord.
²⁴ *Judge me, O God my God, according to thy righteousness;*
And let them not rejoice over me.
²⁵ *Let them not say in their heart, Aha, so would we have it:*
Let them not say, We have swallowed him up.
²⁶ *Let them be put to shame and confounded together*
That rejoice at my hurt:
Let them be clothed with shame and dishonor
That magnify themselves against me.
²⁷ *Let them shout for joy, and be glad, that favor my righteous cause:*
Yea, let them say continually, God be magnified,
Who hath pleasure in the prosperity of his servant.
²⁸ *And my tongue shall talk of thy righteousness*
And of thy praise all the day long.

Our prayers
Are handmaiden to revenge
Our Psalms
Sing of destruction to our enemies
Expecting a sky god
To protect us from harm
Asking angels
To rise up on our behalf.
As we remember
Incense and expletives

Surrounding barbarians rape the innocent
They tear apart the weak
As if the world we know
Is but a phase
Between Heaven
And Hell

The god of our people
Has abandoned us
Despite cathedrals
And synagogues
And temples to his holy name

Our prayers have gone unanswered
We humble ourselves with sackcloth and ashes
We fast
We meditate on the mysteries
We are met with evil
And mockery
As you look on
If you are even there

We give thanks
For powers we have yet to use
Of peacemaking
Compassion
And universal love
As we come to terms
With who we really are

Yes, we are the children of light

Psalm Thirty-six

1 The transgression of the wicked saith within my heart,
There is no fear of God before his eyes.
² For he flattereth himself in his own eyes,
That his iniquity will not be found out and be hated.
³ The words of his mouth are iniquity and deceit:
He hath ceased to be wise and to do good.
⁴ He deviseth iniquity upon his bed;
He setteth himself in a way that is not good;
He abhorreth not evil.
⁵ Thy loving kindness, O God, is in the heavens;
Thy faithfulness reacheth unto the skies.
⁶ Thy righteousness is like the mountains of God;
Thy judgments are a great deep:
O God, thou preservest man and beast.
⁷ How precious is thy loving kindness, O God!
And the children of men take refuge under the shadow of thy wings.
⁸ They shall be abundantly satisfied with the fatness of thy house;
And thou wilt make them drink of the river of thy pleasures.
⁹ For with thee is the fountain of life:
In thy light shall we see light.
¹⁰ Oh continue thy loving kindness unto them that know thee,
And thy righteousness to the upright in heart.
¹¹ Let not the foot of pride come against me,
And let not the hand of the wicked drive me away.
¹² There are the workers of iniquity fallen:
They are thrust down, and shall not be able to rise.

What do we say about a leader
Who lies?
Whose central frame of reference remains himself?
Can we call him wicked in the language of the Psalms
Or maybe call a psychiatrist
To possibly prescribe

Some kind of meds?

Surely the Holy Ghost
The commanding Spirit of
All that is Holy and Good
Will lead this errant gentleman
Out of the furnace of insanity
And self-regard
Into a more comprehensive world

Or maybe not

The universe
Protects cobras and mambas
Sting rays and polar bears
It serves up
Volcanic eruptions
That bury whole tribes in radioactive sludge
Not to be uncovered for a thousand years

Hyenas prowl with impunity
Hitlers come and go
Murdering millions
Destroying libraries and children
Whichever might come first

And leaders lie
Despite us

One day, millennia from now,
We will understand the strength of our hearts
And our hunger to love our own
And that sense of ourselves
Will override
The surrounding wilderness

Not now
Not now

Psalm Thirty-seven

1 Fret not thyself because of evil-doers,
Neither be thou envious against them that work unrighteousness.
² For they shall soon be cut down like the grass,
And wither as the green herb.
³ Trust in God, and do good;
Dwell in the land, and feed on his faithfulness.
⁴ Delight thyself also in God;
And he will give thee the desires of thy heart.
⁵ Commit thy way unto God;
Trust also in him, and he will bring it to pass.
⁶ And he will make thy righteousness to go forth as the light,
And thy justice as the noon-day.
⁷ Rest in God, and wait patiently for him:
Fret not thyself because of him who prospereth in his way,
Because of the man who bringeth wicked devices to pass.
⁸ Cease from anger, and forsake wrath:
Fret not thyself, it tendeth only to evil-doing.
⁹ For evil-doers shall be cut off;
But those that wait for God, they shall inherit the land.
¹⁰ For yet a little while, and the wicked shall not be:
Yea, thou shalt diligently consider his place, and he shall not be.
¹¹ But the meek shall inherit the land,
And shall delight themselves in the abundance of peace.
¹² The wicked plotteth against the just,
And gnasheth upon him with his teeth.
¹³ The Lord will laugh at him;
For he seeth that his day is coming.
¹⁴ The wicked have drawn out the sword, and have bent their bow,
To cast down the poor and needy,
To slay such as are upright in the way.
¹⁵ Their sword shall enter into their own heart,
And their bows shall be broken.
¹⁶ Better is a little that the righteous hath

Than the abundance of many wicked.
[17] For the arms of the wicked shall be broken;
But God upholdeth the righteous.
[18] God knoweth the days of the perfect;
And their inheritance shall be for ever.
[19] They shall not be put to shame in the time of evil;
And in the days of famine they shall be satisfied.
[20] But the wicked shall perish,
And the enemies of God shall be as the fat of lambs:
They shall consume; in smoke shall they consume away.
[21] The wicked borroweth, and payeth not again;
But the righteous dealeth graciously, and giveth.
[22] For such as are blessed of him shall inherit the land;
And they that are cursed of him shall be cut off.
[23] A man's goings are established of God;
And he delighteth in his way.
[24] Though he fall, he shall not be utterly cast down;
For God upholdeth him with his hand.
[25] I have been young, and now am old;
Yet have I not seen the righteous forsaken,
Nor his seed begging bread.
[26] All the day long he dealeth graciously, and lendeth;
And his seed is blessed.
[27] Depart from evil, and do good;
And dwell for evermore.
[28] For God loveth justice,
And forsaketh not his saints;
They are preserved for ever:
But the seed of the wicked shall be cut off.
[29] The righteous shall inherit the land,
And dwell therein for ever.
[30] The mouth of the righteous talketh of wisdom,
And his tongue speaketh justice.
[31] The law of his God is in his heart;
None of his steps shall slide.
[32] The wicked watcheth the righteous,

And seeketh to slay him.
[33] God will not leave him in his hand,
Nor condemn him when he is judged.
[34] Wait for God, and keep his way,
And he will exalt thee to inherit the land:
When the wicked are cut off, thou shalt see it.
[35] I have seen the wicked in great power,
And spreading himself like a green tree in its native soil.
[36] But one passed by, and, lo, he was not:
Yea, I sought him, but he could not be found.
[37] Mark the perfect man, and behold the upright;
For there is a happy end to the man of peace.
[38] As for transgressors, they shall be destroyed together:
The end of the wicked shall be cut off.
[39] But the salvation of the righteous is of God:
He is their stronghold in the time of trouble.
[40] And God helpeth them, and rescueth them:
He rescueth them from the wicked, and saveth them,
Because they have taken refuge in him.

The day is coming
When oh
We stop dividing the world
Into good and bad
Light and dark
Us and them

When we stop demonizing enemies
When we ask forgiveness
For enslaving mostly Africans
Let's be specific here

That's how love begins:
In the details

And moving right along
Slaughtering the indigenous
Sorry
They weren't slaughtered
The Indians died of disease
Don't you know anything?

When will we forgive the barbarians
Who raped and murdered our very own
Causing multi-generational shame
And confusion
Erasing memory and desire?

The day is coming
When thoughts and prayers
And trusting in a so-called God
Yield to our innate ability
To restore the natural world
And transform its human tribe

Cease from anger
Proclaims the ancient Lord of All

Somewhere in the ethers
Between the fantasy
And the dream
Will come cease-fire
And the end of war

The day is coming
Bringing light

We will grant mercy
And do good

That day is coming soon

Psalm Thirty-eight

1 O God, rebuke me not in thy wrath;
Neither chasten me in thy hot displeasure.
² For thine arrows stick fast in me,
And thy hand presseth me sore.
³ There is no soundness in my flesh because of thine indignation;
Neither is there any health in my bones because of my sin.
⁴ For mine iniquities are gone over my head:
As a heavy burden they are too heavy for me.
⁵ My wounds are loathsome and corrupt,
Because of my foolishness.
⁶ I am pained and bowed down greatly;
I go mourning all the day long.
⁷ For my loins are filled with burning;
And there is no soundness in my flesh.
⁸ I am faint and sore bruised:
I have groaned by reason of the disquietness of my heart.
⁹ Lord, all my desire is before thee;
And my groaning is not hid from thee.
¹⁰ My heart throbbeth, my strength faileth me:
As for the light of mine eyes, it also is gone from me.
¹¹ My lovers and my friends stand aloof from my plague;
And my kinsmen stand afar off.
¹² They also that seek after my life lay snares for me;
And they that seek my hurt speak mischievous things,
And meditate deceits all the day long.
¹³ But I, as a deaf man, hear not;
And I am as a dumb man that openeth not his mouth.
¹⁴ Yea, I am as a man that heareth not,
And in whose mouth are no reproofs.
¹⁵ For in thee, O God, do I hope:
Thou wilt answer, O Lord my God.
¹⁶ For I said, Lest they rejoice over me:
When my foot slippeth, they magnify themselves against me.

¹⁷ *For I am ready to fall,*
And my sorrow is continually before me.
¹⁸ *For I will declare mine iniquity;*
I will be sorry for my sin.
¹⁹ *But mine enemies are lively, and are strong;*
And they that hate me wrongfully are multiplied.
²⁰ *They also that render evil for good*
Are adversaries unto me, because I follow the thing that is good.
²¹ *Forsake me not, O God:*
O my God, be not far from me.
²² *Make haste to help me,*
O Lord, my salvation.

Beyond the beyond
I sit below
In the bottom of a pit
Of my own making

Monsters devour my soul

I hold myself responsible
For my own sorry state

How can I blame chemicals
Childhood trauma
Dead parents
And absent friends?

Only I
Have fashioned my personal night
Out of forgotten grief
Not knowing why
I resist
The best of the world
Why I resist
The love all around me
Having little to do
With religion and its ungainly pursuits

I was deaf and could not hear
Blind and could not see
And dumb as dirt

I still hope
Still crave
Still demand
The unbounded love
I sense
And do not know
Except for the hunger
In my core

Why would I long for a God
If there were none?

How could that be?

Is my soul not tuned in
To reality?

Psalm Thirty-nine

1 *I said, I will take heed to my ways,*
That I sin not with my tongue:
I will keep my mouth with a bridle,
While the wicked is before me.
² *I was dumb with silence, I held my peace, even from good;*
And my sorrow was stirred.
³ *My heart was hot within me;*
While I was musing the fire burned;
Then spake I with my tongue:
⁴ *God, make me to know mine end,*
And the measure of my days, what it is;
Let me know how frail I am.
⁵ *Behold, thou hast made my days as handbreadths;*
And my life-time is as nothing before thee:
Surely every man at his best estate is altogether vanity.
⁶ *Surely every man walketh in a vain show;*
Surely they are disquieted in vain:
He heapeth up riches, and knoweth not who shall gather them.
⁷ *And now, Lord, what wait I for?*
My hope is in thee.
⁸ *Deliver me from all my transgressions:*
Make me not the reproach of the foolish.
⁹ *I was dumb, I opened not my mouth;*
Because thou didst it.
¹⁰ *Remove thy stroke away from me:*
I am consumed by the blow of thy hand.
¹¹ *When thou with rebukes dost correct man for iniquity,*
Thou makest his beauty to consume away like a moth:
Surely every man is vanity.
¹² *Hear my prayer, O God, and give ear unto my cry;*
Hold not thy peace at my tears:
For I am a stranger with thee,
A sojourner, as all my fathers were.

*¹³ Oh spare me, that I may recover strength,
Before I go hence, and be no more.*

I'm a good girl, I am
Said Eliza Doolittle
The Cockney flower girl
Barely intelligible at times
And certainly silent
Before she learned to speak
Among her betters
And hold her own
With the aristocrats

And for what?

As for myself
I stand mute before the Universe
Imagining I have transgressed
But don't know how

Born empty of heart
Imaging a Lord
Who will forgive me for being alive

I have the power to choose
They say
Choose what?
What man dare choose evil
And despair?

I am a stranger unto myself
I come from wanderers

Whoever you are
Hear my prayer
Before I disappear
And am no more

Psalm Forty

1 I waited patiently for God;
And he inclined unto me, and heard my cry.
² He brought me up also out of a horrible pit, out of the miry clay;
And he set my feet upon a rock, and established my goings.
³ And he hath put a new song in my mouth, even praise unto our God:
Many shall see it, and fear,
And shall trust in God.
⁴ Blessed is the man that maketh God his trust,
And respecteth not the proud, nor such as turn aside to lies.
⁵ Many, O God my God, are the wonderful works
Which thou hast done,
And thy thoughts which are to us-ward:
They cannot be set in order unto thee;
If I would declare and speak of them,
They are more than can be numbered.
⁶ Sacrifice and offering thou hast no delight in;
Mine ears hast thou opened:
Burnt-offering and sin-offering hast thou not required.
⁷ Then said I, Lo, I am come;
In the roll of the book it is written of me:
⁸ I delight to do thy will, O my God;
Yea, thy law is within my heart.
⁹ I have proclaimed glad tidings of righteousness in the great assembly;
Lo, I will not refrain my lips,
O God, thou knowest.
¹⁰ I have not hid thy righteousness within my heart;
I have declared thy faithfulness and thy salvation;
I have not concealed thy loving kindness
And thy truth from the great assembly.
¹¹ Withhold not thou thy tender mercies from me, O God;
Let thy loving kindness and thy truth continually preserve me.
¹² For innumerable evils have compassed me about;
Mine iniquities have overtaken me, so that I am not able to look up;

They are more than the hairs of my head;
And my heart hath failed me.
¹³ Be pleased, O God, to deliver me:
Make haste to help me, O God.
¹⁴ Let them be put to shame and confounded together
That seek after my soul to destroy it:
Let them be turned backward and brought to dishonor
That delight in my hurt.
¹⁵ Let them be desolate by reason of their shame
That say unto me, Aha, aha.
¹⁶ Let all those that seek thee rejoice and be glad in thee:
Let such as love thy salvation say continually,
God be magnified.
¹⁷ But I am poor and needy;
Yet the Lord thinketh upon me:
Thou art my help and my deliverer;
Make no tarrying, O my God.

I have been given songs
And unsuspecting beauty
Hurricanes
Ferocious in their majesty
Eagles in the sky
Women possessed of boundless love
Blessed be the earth
And birth continual

The sound of color
Fragments of laughter
Defeating death

We open like flowers
Dazzling for a day
And afterwards
Petals fall
One after the other
Into the primeval fire

We ask for deliverance
From those who wish to destroy us
As we rejoice
In simple things

Psalm Forty-one

1 Blessed is he that considereth the poor:
God will deliver him in the day of evil.
² God will preserve him, and keep him alive,
And he shall be blessed upon the earth;
And deliver not thou him unto the will of his enemies.
³ God will support him upon the couch of languishing:
Thou makest all his bed in his sickness.
⁴ I said, O God, have mercy upon me:
Heal my soul; for I have sinned against thee.
⁵ Mine enemies speak evil against me, saying,
When will he die, and his name perish?
⁶ And if he come to see me, he speaketh falsehood;
His heart gathereth iniquity to itself:
When he goeth abroad, he telleth it.
⁷ All that hate me whisper together against me;
Against me do they devise my hurt.
⁸ An evil disease, say they, cleaveth fast unto him;
And now that he lieth he shall rise up no more.
⁹ Yea, mine own familiar friend, in whom I trusted,
Who did eat of my bread,
Hath lifted up his heel against me.
¹⁰ But thou, O God, have mercy upon me, and raise me up,
That I may requite them.
¹¹ By this I know that thou delightest in me,
Because mine enemy doth not triumph over me.
¹² And as for me, thou upholdest me in mine integrity,
And settest me before thy face for ever.
¹³ Blessed be God, the God of Israel,
From everlasting and to everlasting.
Amen, and Amen.
Blessed is he that considereth the poor
The Lord will deliver him in time of trouble

Coals to Newcastle
Pouring water into the sea
Pick your metaphor

The Lord delivers no one
Raise your hands in the air
You neighborhood organizers
And soup kitchen democrats
Before the tax man comes

Or somebody says you're holding a gun
And that's the end of you

> *The poor ye shall have always among you*

Who said that?
The only deliverance for caregivers
The morgue

Cynicism arrives after millennia of prayer

Nothing changes nothing
But invention
And technology

And ever so often love

Bicycles bring women out of the neighborhoods
The Internet creates conversation
Conspiracy
And eventual transparency

Community appears like a summer storm
Wreaking turmoil
And watering the ground

Who did this?
The Lord?

Who created love?

Why do definitions blur before the ink is dry?

Blessed be the Lord God of Israel from everlasting and to everlasting and Amen

Or so they say

Psalm Forty-two

1 As the hart panteth after the water brooks,
So panteth my soul after thee, O God.
2 My soul thirsteth for God, for the living God:
When shall I come and appear before God?
3 My tears have been my food day and night,
While they continually say unto me, Where is thy God?
4 These things I remember, and pour out my soul within me,
How I went with the throng, and led them to the house of God,
With the voice of joy and praise, a multitude keeping holyday.
5 Why art thou cast down, O my soul?
And why art thou disquieted within me?
Hope thou in God; for I shall yet praise him
For the help of his countenance.
6 O my God, my soul is cast down within me:
Therefore do I remember thee from the land of the Jordan,
And the Hermons, from the hill Mizar.
7 Deep calleth unto deep at the noise of thy waterfalls:
All thy waves and thy billows are gone over me.
8 Yet God will command his loving kindness in the day-time;
And in the night his song shall be with me,
Even a prayer unto the God of my life.
9 I will say unto God my rock, Why hast thou forgotten me?
Why go I mourning because of the oppression of the enemy?
10 As with a sword in my bones, mine adversaries reproach me,
While they continually say unto me, Where is thy God?
11 Why art thou cast down, O my soul?
And why art thou disquieted within me?
Hope thou in God; for I shall yet praise him,
Who is the help of my countenance, and my God.

People ask
Where do you worship

Meaning
Where you go to church?
We say
Every place

That don't do it

They say
Why don't you believe?

We say we believe
We believe

In what?

They want a picture of our god
That would be Jesus, Buddha, Moses
What about Mary Immaculate?
How about Zeus
Someone connected to the sky?

Habitual people
Don't feel confident
'round people like us
Who don't put cash in the collection plate

Do I thirst after God like it say?
Why should I believe?
Why is my soul cast down?

Tell me, Soul
Who are you?
Why are you silent?
Where have you been?

Deep calleth unto deep
Tell me, Soul
Where have you been?

Who be you be?

Psalm Forty–three

1 Judge me, O God, and plead my cause against an ungodly nation:
Oh deliver me from the deceitful and unjust man.
² For thou art the God of my strength; why hast thou cast me off?
Why go I mourning because of the oppression of the enemy?
³ Oh send out thy light and thy truth; let them lead me:
Let them bring me unto thy holy hill,
And to thy tabernacles.
⁴ Then will I go unto the altar of God,
Unto God my exceeding joy;
And upon the harp will I praise thee, O God, my God.
⁵ Why art thou cast down, O my soul?
And why art thou disquieted within me?
Hope thou in God; for I shall yet praise him,
Who is the help of my countenance, and my God.

Deliver us from
Deliberate people
Who mysteriously make money
Off everything they touch

Deliver us from
Everyone who takes a percentage
Off every deal
Every contract
Every breath
Every baby born to humankind

The sharpies
The hustlers
The scammers
The crooks
Who buy their suits
In Saville Row
Right-o

Our enemies
The word no long applies
Only the weapons
No longer carry broadswords
And pikes
No Winchester 73s

These days
Our enemies
Control the light
And the light switch

They kill with a flick of the pen
And the umbrella

As we pray to the Lord
Or whoever hears our prayers
and praise him upon the harp

Which these days
Sits in the corner
Not making a sound

Psalm Forty-four

1 *We have heard with our ears, O God,*
Our fathers have told us,
What work thou didst in their days,
In the days of old.
² *Thou didst drive out the nations with thy hand;*
But them thou didst plant:
Thou didst afflict the peoples;
But them thou didst spread abroad.
³ *For they gat not the land in possession by their own sword,*
Neither did their own arm save them;
But thy right hand, and thine arm, and the light of thy countenance,
Because thou wast favorable unto them.
⁴ *Thou art my King, O God:*
Command deliverance for Jacob
⁵ *Through thee will we push down our adversaries:*
Through thy name will we tread them under that rise up against us.
⁶ *For I will not trust in my bow,*
Neither shall my sword save me.
⁷ *But thou hast saved us from our adversaries,*
And hast put them to shame that hate us.
⁸ *In God have we made our boast all the day long,*
And we will give thanks unto thy name for ever.
⁹ *But now thou hast cast us off, and brought us to dishonor,*
And goest not forth with our hosts.
¹⁰ *Thou makest us to turn back from the adversary;*
And they that hate us take spoil for themselves.
¹¹ *Thou hast made us like sheep appointed for food,*
And hast scattered us among the nations.
¹² *Thou sellest thy people for nought,*
And hast not increased thy wealth by their price.
¹³ *Thou makest us a reproach to our neighbors,*
A scoffing and a derision to them that are round about us.
¹⁴ *Thou makest us a byword among the nations,*

A shaking of the head among the peoples.
¹⁵ *All the day long is my dishonor before me,*
And the shame of my face hath covered me,
¹⁶ *For the voice of him that reproacheth and blasphemeth,*
By reason of the enemy and the avenger.
¹⁷ *All this is come upon us; yet have we not forgotten thee,*
Neither have we dealt falsely in thy covenant.
¹⁸ *Our heart is not turned back,*
Neither have our steps declined from thy way,
¹⁹ *That thou hast sore broken us in the place of jackals,*
And covered us with the shadow of death.
²⁰ *If we have forgotten the name of our God,*
Or spread forth our hands to a strange god;
²¹ *Will not God search this out?*
For he knoweth the secrets of the heart.
²² *Yea, for thy sake are we killed all the day long;*
We are accounted as sheep for the slaughter.
²³ *Awake, why sleepest thou, O LORD?*
Arise, cast us not off for ever.
²⁴ *Wherefore hidest thou thy face,*
And forgettest our affliction and our oppression?
²⁵ *For our soul is bowed down to the dust:*
Our body cleaveth unto the earth.
²⁶ *Rise up for our help,*
And redeem us for thy loving kindness' sake.

I no longer trust in the hydrogen bomb
Or intercontinental missiles

Do you?

We live in uncertainty
And dread
Once again
Awaiting destruction
And lingering disgrace

Death comes round in Spring
And then again
In Summer
Winter
Fall
Is there anything left?

Where are you
When the sky turns red
And the air disappears
And shame becomes our daily bread?

Have you forgotten us?

Wake up!
Rejoice in us!
As we rejoice in you
You know the secrets of our hearts

Do not forget us
At least
Not before
We forget ourselves

And by default
Abandon you.

Psalm Forty-five

1 My heart overfloweth with a goodly matter;
I speak the things which I have made touching the king:
My tongue is the pen of a ready writer.
² Thou art fairer than the children of men;
Grace is poured into thy lips:
Therefore God hath blessed thee for ever.
³ Gird thy sword upon thy thigh, O mighty one,
Thy glory and thy majesty.
⁴ And in thy majesty ride on prosperously,
Because of truth and meekness and righteousness:
And thy right hand shall teach thee terrible things.
⁵ Thine arrows are sharp;
The peoples fall under thee;
They are in the heart of the king's enemies.
⁶ Thy throne, O God, is for ever and ever:
A sceptre of equity is the sceptre of thy kingdom.
⁷ Thou hast loved righteousness, and hated wickedness:
Therefore God, thy God, hath anointed thee
With the oil of gladness above thy fellows.
⁸ All thy garments smell of myrrh, and aloes, and cassia;
Out of ivory palaces stringed instruments have made thee glad.
⁹ Kings' daughters are among thy honorable women:
At thy right hand doth stand the queen in gold of Ophir.
¹⁰ Hearken, O daughter, and consider, and incline thine ear;
Forget also thine own people, and thy father's house:
¹¹ So will the king desire thy beauty;
For he is thy lord; and reverence thou him.
¹² And the daughter of Tyre shall be there with a gift;
The rich among the people shall entreat thy favor.
¹³ The king's daughter within the palace is all glorious:
Her clothing is inwrought with gold.
¹⁴ She shall be led unto the king in broidered work:
The virgins her companions that follow her

Shall be brought unto thee.
¹⁵ With gladness and rejoicing shall they be led:
They shall enter into the king's palace.
¹⁶ Instead of thy fathers shall be thy children,
Whom thou shalt make princes in all the earth.
¹⁷ I will make thy name to be remembered in all generations:
Therefore shall the peoples give thee thanks for ever and ever.

Do we confuse kings and God?
Guess what?
Kings are going out of style
Which is to say
Obliterated
And erased

We the peasantry
No longer wish
To be summarily subjected to
The Divine Right of Monsters
Wearing crowns
And subterranean IQs

Look beyond
Bolsheviks
The Cultural Revolution
The firing squads and crematoria
Of self-made emperors
Whose names now lurk in our collective DNA

O God
Whoever you may be
Are you not more powerful than tsars?
More nurturing than executioners?

Who are these daughters
The psalmist sings about
With gladness and rejoicing
Wearing garments made of gold?

Who are your children
You will make princes once again?

Where are we going
With this misnaming
Of who we be
This dysfunctional
Chain of command?

How much more slaughter
Must we endure
Before we understand you
In different terms
Than palaces and crowns?

And whose bloody fault is that?

Psalm Forty–six

1 God is our refuge and strength,
A very present help in trouble.
² Therefore will we not fear, though the earth do change,
And though the mountains be shaken into the heart of the seas;
³ Though the waters thereof roar and be troubled,
Though the mountains tremble with the swelling thereof.
⁴ There is a river, the streams whereof make glad the city of God,
The holy place of the tabernacles of the Most High.
⁵ God is in the midst of her; she shall not be moved:
God will help her, and that right early.
⁶ The nations raged, the kingdoms were moved:
He uttered his voice, the earth melted.
⁷ God of hosts is with us;
The God of Jacob is our refuge.
⁸ Come, behold the works of God,
What desolations he hath made in the earth.
⁹ He maketh wars to cease unto the end of the earth;
He breaketh the bow, and cutteth the spear in sunder;
He burneth the chariots in the fire.
¹⁰ Be still, and know that I am God:
I will be exalted among the nations, I will be exalted in the earth.
¹¹ God of hosts is with us;
The God of Jacob is our refuge.

Be still and know that I am God
Whispers the voice
Within my hurricane

My heart
surrounded by psychopaths
Who feast on death

I call on the name
Of someone beyond myself
Someone I have only imagined
Who judges history
And the works of men

Most of whom
Worship the world
And little else
Idols
Money
Various monarchies
And Academy Awards

Psalm Forty-seven

1 Oh clap your hands, all ye peoples;
Shout unto God with the voice of triumph.
² For God Most High is terrible;
He is a great King over all the earth.
³ He subdueth peoples under us,
And nations under our feet.
⁴ He chooseth our inheritance for us,
The glory of Jacob whom he loved.
⁵ God is gone up with a shout,
God with the sound of a trumpet.
⁶ Sing praises to God, sing praises:
Sing praises unto our King, sing praises.
⁷ For God is the King of all the earth:
Sing ye praises with understanding.
⁸ God reigneth over the nations:
God sitteth upon his holy throne.
⁹ The princes of the peoples are gathered together
To be the people of the God of Abraham;
For the shields of the earth belong unto God:
He is greatly exalted.

Clap your hands
Y'all
Shout with the voice of victory
Decide exactly who you are

Whatever you do
Dammit
Sing!
Fill the air
With sound
And melody

Praise life
And when you do
You will start to know
The beginning of joy

Psalm Forty-eight

1 Great is God, and greatly to be praised,
In the city of our God, in his holy mountain.
² Beautiful in elevation, the joy of the whole earth,
Is mount Zion, on the sides of the north,
The city of the great King.
³ God hath made himself known in her palaces for a refuge.
⁴ For, lo, the kings assembled themselves,
They passed by together.
⁵ They saw it, then were they amazed;
They were dismayed, they hasted away.
⁶ Trembling took hold of them there,
Pain, as of a woman in travail.
⁷ With the east wind
Thou breakest the ships of Tarshish.
⁸ As we have heard, so have we seen
In the city of God of hosts, in the city of our God:
God will establish it for ever.
⁹ We have thought on thy loving kindness, O God,
In the midst of thy temple.
¹⁰ As is thy name, O God,
So is thy praise unto the ends of the earth:
Thy right hand is full of righteousness.
¹¹ Let mount Zion be glad,
Let the daughters of Judah rejoice,
Because of thy judgments.
¹² Walk about Zion, and go round about her;
Number the towers thereof;
¹³ Mark ye well her bulwarks;
Consider her palaces:
That ye may tell it to the generation following.
¹⁴ For this God is our God for ever and ever:
He will be our guide even unto death.

Great is the Lord
If we can locate him or her or it
Beyond name
And title
Beyond our sense
Of what we call divine
Beyond number
And weight
Beyond matter
Beyond history

Great is the mind
That rules
A trillion stars

Great is the heart
That rules
The love
We barely know

Or understand

Psalm Forty-nine

1 Hear this, all ye peoples;
Give ear, all ye inhabitants of the world,
² Both low and high,
Rich and poor together.
³ My mouth shall speak wisdom;
And the meditation of my heart shall be of understanding.
⁴ I will incline mine ear to a parable:
I will open my dark saying upon the harp.
⁵ Wherefore should I fear in the days of evil,
When iniquity at my heels compasseth me about?
⁶ They that trust in their wealth,
And boast themselves in the multitude of their riches;
⁷ None of them can by any means redeem his brother,
Nor give to God a ransom for him
⁸ (For the redemption of their life is costly,
And it faileth for ever),
⁹ That he should still live alway,
That he should not see corruption.
¹⁰ For he shall see it. Wise men die;
The fool and the brutish alike perish,
And leave their wealth to others.
¹¹ Their inward thought is, that their houses shall continue for ever,
And their dwelling-places to all generations;
They call their lands after their own names.
¹² But man being in honor abideth not:
He is like the beasts that perish.
¹³ This their way is their folly:
Yet after them men approve their sayings. Selah
¹⁴ They are appointed as a flock for Sheol;
Death shall be their shepherd:
And the upright shall have dominion over them in the morning;
And their beauty shall be for Sheol to consume,
That there be no habitation for it.

*15 But God will redeem my soul from the power of Sheol;
For he will receive me. Selah
16 Be not thou afraid when one is made rich,
When the glory of his house is increased:
17 For when he dieth he shall carry nothing away;
His glory shall not descend after him.
18 Though while he lived he blessed his soul
(And men praise thee, when thou doest well to thyself),
19 He shall go to the generation of his fathers;
They shall never see the light.
20 Man that is in honor, and understandeth not,
Is like the beasts that perish.*

Nobody has much good to say
About the nouveau riche.
Not then
Not now

Poor babies
Obsessed with "things"
Is the usual complaint
One tinged with contempt
For supposed bad taste
Imagining houses
And limousines
And marble statues of the gods
Will last forever
When the fact is
As we well do understand
We are standing on the edge of death

Or as some would have it
The Universe

Yes, death will consume us
Big surprise
And then what?

We can only hope
The Creative Source
Of All That Is

Will notice us
As we slumber in our graves
And will raise us up
Despite our terrible taste in interior design
Gold plated limousines
and Gods
At least
That's the particular conceit

Psalm Fifty

1 The Mighty One, God, hath spoken,
And called the earth from the rising of the sun
Unto the going down thereof.
² Out of Zion, the perfection of beauty,
God hath shined forth.
³ Our God cometh, and doth not keep silence:
A fire devoureth before him,
And it is very tempestuous round about him.
⁴ He calleth to the heavens above,
And to the earth, that he may judge his people:
⁵ Gather my saints together unto me,
Those that have made a covenant with me by sacrifice.
⁶ And the heavens shall declare his righteousness;
For God is judge himself.
⁷ Hear, O my people, and I will speak;
O Israel, and I will testify unto thee:
I am God, even thy God.
⁸ I will not reprove thee for thy sacrifices;
And thy burnt-offerings are continually before me.
⁹ I will take no bullock out of thy house,
Nor he-goats out of thy folds.
¹⁰ For every beast of the forest is mine,
And the cattle upon a thousand hills.
¹¹ I know all the birds of the mountains;
And the wild beasts of the field are mine.
¹² If I were hungry, I would not tell thee;
For the world is mine, and the fulness thereof.
¹³ Will I eat the flesh of bulls,
Or drink the blood of goats?
¹⁴ Offer unto God the sacrifice of thanksgiving;
And pay thy vows unto the Most High;
¹⁵ And call upon me in the day of trouble:
I will deliver thee, and thou shalt glorify me.

¹⁶ But unto the wicked God saith,
What hast thou to do to declare my statutes,
And that thou hast taken my covenant in thy mouth,
¹⁷ Seeing that thou hatest instruction,
And castest my words behind thee?
¹⁸ When thou sawest a thief, thou consentedst with him,
And hast been partaker with adulterers.
¹⁹ Thou givest thy mouth to evil,
And thy tongue frameth deceit.
²⁰ Thou sittest and speakest against thy brother;
Thou slanderest thine own mother's son.
²¹ These things hast thou done, and I kept silence;
Thou thoughtest that I was altogether such a one as thyself:
But I will reprove thee, and set them in order before thine eyes.
²² Now consider this, ye that forget God,
Lest I tear you in pieces, and there be none to deliver:
²³ Whoso offereth the sacrifice of thanksgiving glorifieth me;
And to him that ordereth his way aright
Will I show the salvation of God.

We feast on tales of visiting deities
Sky gods who abandoned us
Promising to return

We wait for their pending approach
Call it the Messiah
The Second Coming
Or just whispers
About these self-ordained immortals
And their mothers
Occasionally appearing to children
And to nuns

God will come to judge, they say
Oh good

The word is out:
The flesh of bulls
The blood of goats
The wild beasts of the field
In fact the fields themselves
All belong to God

Call unto him
And he will deliver you

If you forget him
He will tear you to pieces
That's what they tell us

Praise him
Glorify his holy name

Your move

Psalm Fifty-one

1 *Have mercy upon me, O God, according to thy loving kindness:*
According to the multitude of thy tender mercies
Blot out my transgressions.
² *Wash me thoroughly from mine iniquity,*
And cleanse me from my sin.
³ *For I know my transgressions;*
And my sin is ever before me.
⁴ *Against thee, thee only, have I sinned,*
And done that which is evil in thy sight;
That thou mayest be justified when thou speakest,
And be clear when thou judgest.
⁵ *Behold, I was brought forth in iniquity;*
And in sin did my mother conceive me.
⁶ *Behold, thou desirest truth in the inward parts;*
And in the hidden part thou wilt make me to know wisdom.
⁷ *Purify me with hyssop, and I shall be clean:*
Wash me, and I shall be whiter than snow.
⁸ *Make me to hear joy and gladness,*
That the bones which thou hast broken may rejoice.
⁹ *Hide thy face from my sins,*
And blot out all mine iniquities.
¹⁰ *Create in me a clean heart, O God;*
And renew a right spirit within me.
¹¹ *Cast me not away from thy presence;*
And take not thy holy Spirit from me.
¹² *Restore unto me the joy of thy salvation;*
And uphold me with a willing spirit.
¹³ *Then will I teach transgressors thy ways;*
And sinners shall be converted unto thee.
¹⁴ *Deliver me from bloodguiltiness, O God, thou God of my salvation;*
And my tongue shall sing aloud of thy righteousness.
¹⁵ *O Lord, open thou my lips;*
And my mouth shall show forth thy praise.

¹⁶ *For thou delightest not in sacrifice; else would I give it:*
Thou hast no pleasure in burnt-offering.
¹⁷ *The sacrifices of God are a broken spirit:*
A broken and a contrite heart, O God, thou wilt not despise.
¹⁸ *Do good in thy good pleasure unto Zion:*
Build thou the walls of Jerusalem.
¹⁹ *Then wilt thou delight in the sacrifices of righteousness,*
In burnt-offering and whole burnt-offering:
Then will they offer bullocks upon thine altar.

A broken heart
Is the beginning of wisdom

A worn-out soul
hears
the silence
Of God

A shattered spirit
Lies dead in the night
Only to rise into the light
When there is nothing else
And yet we wonder
Who is this God
We grovel in front of
This tribal deity we beg forgiveness from?

We ask him to cleanse us
To deliver us into praise and jubilation
And restore our joy

As we expect him
To destroy our enemies
Whoever we say they are

Surely
We have not yet begun to know
This life

Beyond face and form
Beyond good and evil
And happy endings

We are created in the image of him
They say

No, we are created
In the image of love

And what is that?

You decide

Psalm Fifty-two

1 Why boastest thou thyself in mischief, O mighty man?
The loving kindness of God endureth continually.
² Thy tongue deviseth very wickedness,
Like a sharp razor, working deceitfully.
³ Thou lovest evil more than good,
And lying rather than to speak righteousness. Selah
⁴ Thou lovest all devouring words,
O thou deceitful tongue.
⁵ God will likewise destroy thee for ever;
He will take thee up, and pluck thee out of thy tent,
And root thee out of the land of the living. Selah
⁶ The righteous also shall see it, and fear,
And shall laugh at him, saying,
⁷ Lo, this is the man that made not God his strength,
But trusted in the abundance of his riches,
And strengthened himself in his wickedness.
⁸ But as for me, I am like a green olive-tree in the house of God:
I trust in the loving kindness of God for ever and ever.
⁹ I will give thee thanks for ever, because thou hast done it;
And I will hope in thy name, for it is good, in the presence of thy saints.

Beyond war and execution
Beyond rape
And punishment
Beyond terror
Beyond blasphemy
Which is the worst of sins
Worshipping tribal gods
With faces like our own
We meet mercy
And embrace forgiveness
That's how we've been made

With mercy
We are given the possibility of trust
The goodness that shall follow us
All the days of our lives
Just like we've been told

Green olive trees
Growing strong
In the house of God
You'll see

Psalm Fifty-three

1 The fool hath said in his heart, There is no God.
Corrupt are they, and have done abominable iniquity;
There is none that doeth good.
² God looked down from heaven upon the children of men,
To see if there were any that did understand,
That did seek after God.
³ Every one of them is gone back; they are together become filthy;
There is none that doeth good, no, not one.
⁴ Have the workers of iniquity no knowledge,
Who eat up my people as they eat bread,
And call not upon God?
⁵ There were they in great fear, where no fear was;
For God hath scattered the bones of him that encampeth against thee:
Thou hast put them to shame, because God hath rejected them.
⁶ Oh that the salvation of Israel were come out of Zion!
When God bringeth back the captivity of his people,
Then shall Jacob rejoice, and Israel shall be glad.

We are surrounded by fools
Who see no good in anyone
Except themselves

We are overrun with holocausts
Millions starved, gassed, hanged, burned without end
All for the future
Say the executioners
All for the glorious age to come

Who among us believes
In the holiness of red-haired
Black-skinned, green-eyed humankind
Not to mention beagles
Boykin spaniels, Chihuahuas
Maine coon cats, hippopotami

Irises, petit pois, willow oaks, cottonmouths
Alligators, the Congaree
All things breathing, buzzing, full
Creatures appropriate to earth
Air, marshland, mountains, manmade lakes
Oceans aware
And everywhere

How then can we call upon the unknown God
When the known deity
At least the imagined one
The one we assert is definite and real
Our God we say
Allows overbearing predators
To call upon his holy name
As they swallow up the tired and helpless
Disregard the weak and poor
Mock the innocent
And wreck the earth

Time to reconsider everything
Isn't it?

Amen

Psalm Fifty-four

1 Save me, O God, by thy name,
And judge me in thy might.
² Hear my prayer, O God;
Give ear to the words of my mouth.
³ For strangers are risen up against me,
And violent men have sought after my soul:
They have not set God before them.
⁴ Behold, God is my helper:
The Lord is of them that uphold my soul.
⁵ He will requite the evil unto mine enemies:
Destroy thou them in thy truth.
⁶ With a freewill-offering will I sacrifice unto thee:
I will give thanks unto thy name, O God, for it is good.
⁷ For he hath delivered me out of all trouble;
And mine eye hath seen my desire upon mine enemies.

What is the source of our strength?
We are a nation living with
Fibromyalgia
Bipolar
Moderate schizophrenia
Prescription pills

Don't forget your lithium
Makers Mark
Smirnoff
Johnny Walker Red

The widespread worship of resumes
And wealth
Don't spend the principle
Whose house is it anyway?
The question today:
To whom do we pray?

We are surrounded by enemies
Especially in cyberspace
We have no gates
Or moats
Or battering rams

We have no secrets
Except in the CIA

And the Confessional box
Now out of date
Like sin

The mother planet
Erupts in floods
Tornados
Hurricanes
Who will rescue us?

Where is Hera?
Gaia?
Mother Nature?
Have you seen Minerva?
Where is Mary Immaculate?
For that matter,
Where is Princess Grace?

Otherwise
What's the point?

Capeesh?

Psalm Fifty-five

1 Give ear to my prayer, O God;
And hide not thyself from my supplication.
² Attend unto me, and answer me:
I am restless in my complaint, and moan,
³ Because of the voice of the enemy,
Because of the oppression of the wicked;
For they cast iniquity upon me,
And in anger they persecute me.
⁴ My heart is sore pained within me:
And the terrors of death are fallen upon me.
⁵ Fearfulness and trembling are come upon me,
And horror hath overwhelmed me.
⁶ And I said, Oh that I had wings like a dove!
Then would I fly away, and be at rest.
⁷ Lo, then would I wander far off,
I would lodge in the wilderness.
⁸ I would haste me to a shelter
From the stormy wind and tempest.
⁹ Destroy, O Lord, and divide their tongue;
For I have seen violence and strife in the city.
¹⁰ Day and night they go about it upon the walls thereof:
Iniquity also and mischief are in the midst of it.
¹¹ Wickedness is in the midst thereof:
Oppression and guile depart not from its streets.
¹² For it was not an enemy that reproached me;
Then I could have borne it:
Neither was it he that hated me that did magnify himself against me;
Then I would have hid myself from him:
¹³ But it was thou, a man mine equal,
My companion, and my familiar friend.
¹⁴ We took sweet counsel together;
We walked in the house of God with the throng.
¹⁵ Let death come suddenly upon them,

Let them go down alive into Sheol;
For wickedness is in their dwelling, in the midst of them.
[16] *As for me, I will call upon God;*
And God will save me.
[17] *Evening, and morning, and at noonday, will I complain, and moan;*
And he will hear my voice.
[18] *He hath redeemed my soul in peace from the battle*
That was against me;
For they were many that strove with me.
[19] *God will hear, and answer them,*
Even he that abideth of old, Selah
The men who have no changes,
And who fear not God.
[20] *He hath put forth his hands against such as were at peace with him:*
He hath profaned his covenant.
[21] *His mouth was smooth as butter,*
But his heart was war:
His words were softer than oil,
Yet were they drawn swords.
[22] *Cast thy burden upon God, and he will sustain thee:*
He will never suffer the righteous to be moved.
[23] *But thou, O God, wilt bring them down into the pit of destruction:*
Bloodthirsty and deceitful men shall not live out half their days;
But I will trust in thee.

I want a God to listen to
Whatever nonsense I complain about
Weather
Taxes
Death
Nothwithstanding
Everyone who lies to me
Cheats me
And makes fun of me

When I am done

With my casual complaints
I want this God
To obliterate mine enemies
Cut off their faces
Crush them into the ground
I want him
To annihilate their very souls

With that
I will no longer
lie awake at night
Trembling
Waiting for strangers to break in
And slaughter me

 I will call upon my God
And my God will rescue me

After all
That's what Gods do

Don't they?

Let death seize upon mine enemies
I will call upon my God
He will bring them down
Into the pit of destruction
And I will be comforted

That's what Gods are for

They say

Psalm Fifty-six

1 Be merciful unto me, O God; for man would swallow me up:
All the day long he fighting oppresseth me.
² Mine enemies would swallow me up all the day long;
For they are many that fight proudly against me.
³ What time I am afraid,
I will put my trust in thee.
⁴ In God (I will praise his word),
In God have I put my trust, I will not be afraid;
What can flesh do unto me?
⁵ All the day long they wrest my words:
All their thoughts are against me for evil.
⁶ They gather themselves together, they hide themselves,
They mark my steps,
Even as they have waited for my soul.
⁷ Shall they escape by iniquity?
In anger cast down the peoples, O God.
⁸ Thou numberest my wanderings:
Put thou my tears into thy bottle;
Are they not in thy book?
⁹ Then shall mine enemies turn back in the day that I call:
This I know, that God is for me.
¹⁰ In God (I will praise his word),
In God (I will praise his word),
¹¹ In God have I put my trust, I will not be afraid;
What can man do unto me?
¹² Thy vows are upon me, O God:
I will render thank-offerings unto thee.
¹³ For thou hast delivered my soul from death:
Hast thou not delivered my feet from falling,
That I may walk before God
In the light of the living?

Enemies are the trickiest thing to figure out
They don't seem human
Don't you think?

If anything
They wish to eradicate
Annihilate
Eviscerate
Whatever rhymes with hate
Bait
Wait
Complicate
The best of us

Our museums
The Victoria and Albert
The Tate
MOMA
The Cotton Museum in Bishopsville
Brookgreen Gardens
Our Montessori schools
Baron DeKalb Elementary
Eton
Choate
Central Carolina Technical
They would bomb them all
They've done it before
Wouldn't they?
Enemies
Kaboom

As the Good Book teaches us
We will exterminate every one of them
To protect our children and our heritage

I cry aloud
To the God of our dominions
The Lord of our people
I put my trust in him

He will protect us
From those who are waiting to destroy
Our bodies
And our souls

We will no longer be afraid
God is on our side

How do I know?

The Bible told me so

Psalm Fifty-seven

1 Be merciful unto me, O God, be merciful unto me;
For my soul taketh refuge in thee:
Yea, in the shadow of thy wings will I take refuge,
Until these calamities be overpast.
² I will cry unto God Most High,
Unto God that performeth all things for me.
³ He will send from heaven, and save me,
When he that would swallow me up reproacheth; Selah
God will send forth his loving kindness and his truth.
⁴ My soul is among lions;
I lie among them that are set on fire,
Even the sons of men, whose teeth are spears and arrows,
And their tongue a sharp sword.
⁵ Be thou exalted, O God, above the heavens;
Let thy glory be above all the earth.
⁶ They have prepared a net for my steps;
My soul is bowed down:
They have digged a pit before me;
They are fallen into the midst thereof themselves. Selah
⁷ My heart is fixed, O God, my heart is fixed:
I will sing, yea, I will sing praises.
⁸ Awake up, my glory; awake, psaltery and harp:
I myself will awake right early.
⁹ I will give thanks unto thee, O Lord, among the peoples:
I will sing praises unto thee among the nations.
¹⁰ For thy loving kindness is great unto the heavens,
And thy truth unto the skies.
¹¹ Be thou exalted, O God, above the heavens;
Let thy glory be above all the earth.

I awake early
And sing

Of something higher
Purer
Something more filled with light
And beauty
And grace
Than just about anything here

Just the vision of something luminous
Makes everything worthwhile

With light in the darkness
From some place
I have never been
Or have I?
Comes mercy

Comes glory

Comes love

I will sing of that

All that

And call that God

And I am comforted

Psalm Fifty-eight

¹Do ye indeed in silence speak righteousness?
Do ye judge uprightly, O ye sons of men?
² Nay, in heart ye work wickedness;
Ye weigh out the violence of your hands in the earth.
³ The wicked are estranged from the womb:
They go astray as soon as they are born, speaking lies.
⁴ Their poison is like the poison of a serpent:
They are like the deaf adder that stoppeth her ear,
⁵ Which hearkeneth not to the voice of charmers,
Charming never so wisely.
⁶ Break their teeth, O God, in their mouth:
Break out the great teeth of the young lions, O God.
⁷ Let them melt away as water that runneth apace:
When he aimeth his arrows, let them be as though they were cut off.
⁸ Let them be as a snail which melteth and passeth away,
Like the untimely birth of a woman, that hath not seen the sun.
⁹ Before your pots can feel the thorns,
He will take them away with a whirlwind,
The green and the burning alike.
¹⁰ The righteous shall rejoice when he seeth the vengeance:
He shall wash his feet in the blood of the wicked;
¹¹ So that men shall say, Verily there is a reward for the righteous:
Verily there is a God that judgeth in the earth.

Do you believe in evil?

Some say
Bad is but the absence of good

To believe in God
They say
Meditate on the beauty of the world
Listen to birdsong

Watch wildflowers bloom
Consider the seasons
The caress of spring

Huns come in every generation
Murdering children
Ripping apart
The loveliness of girls
Anything that seems too wonderful

We pray for a God
To smash their teeth
And rip out their tongues
We pray for permission
From the Most High
To wash our feet in the blood of the wicked

We pray for that kind of reward
For us
The righteous
And the good

Psalm Fifty-nine

1 Deliver me from mine enemies, O my God:
Set me on high from them that rise up against me.
² Deliver me from the workers of iniquity,
And save me from the bloodthirsty men.
³ For, lo, they lie in wait for my soul;
The mighty gather themselves together against me:
Not for my transgression, nor for my sin, O God.
⁴ They run and prepare themselves without my fault:
Awake thou to help me, and behold.
⁵ Even thou, O God God of hosts, the God of Israel,
Arise to visit all the nations:
Be not merciful to any wicked transgressors.
⁶ They return at evening, they howl like a dog,
And go round about the city.
⁷ Behold, they belch out with their mouth;
Swords are in their lips:
For who, say they, doth hear?
⁸ But thou, O God, wilt laugh at them;
Thou wilt have all the nations in derision.
⁹ Because of his strength I will give heed unto thee;
For God is my high tower.
¹⁰ My God with his loving kindness will meet me:
God will let me see my desire upon mine enemies.
¹¹ Slay them not, lest my people forget:
Scatter them by thy power, and bring them down,
O Lord our shield.
¹² For the sin of their mouth, and the words of their lips,
Let them even be taken in their pride,
And for cursing and lying which they speak.
¹³ Consume them in wrath, consume them,
So that they shall be no more:
And let them know that God ruleth in Jacob,
Unto the ends of the earth.

¹⁴ *And at evening let them return, let them howl like a dog,*
And go round about the city.
¹⁵ *They shall wander up and down for food,*
And tarry all night if they be not satisfied.
¹⁶ *But I will sing of thy strength;*
Yea, I will sing aloud of thy loving kindness in the morning:
For thou hast been my high tower,
And a refuge in the day of my distress.
¹⁷ *Unto thee, O my strength, will I sing praises:*
For God is my high tower, the God of my mercy.

For five millennia
Five thousand years
Fifty centuries
Count 'em
I have beseeched
Yahweh
The war g-d of the Canaanites
To save me from mine enemies

Auschwitz
Treblinka
The lynching trees of Georgia
They evicted me in Skibbereen
Let me freeze in the Ukraine
Not to mention fabulous Siberia
Havana
San Salvador
Johannesburg

Where were you when I called your holy name
O Lord of Hosts?

These days
I have returned to
Zeus
And to Diana
Goddess of the hunt

At least I know
I made them up

With you
Comes the question of evil
Where does it start?
When will it end?

I heard the lords of the earth
Are now invoking Satan
Instead of you
How does that grab you?

Why do I still wait upon thee?
Why do I still sing of thy power
And ask for mercy in the morning?

What do you think?

Assuming you're still there

Psalm Sixty

1 O God thou hast cast us off, thou hast broken us down;
Thou hast been angry; oh restore us again.
² Thou hast made the land to tremble; thou hast rent it:
Heal the breaches thereof; for it shaketh.
³ Thou hast showed thy people hard things:
Thou hast made us to drink the wine of staggering.
⁴ Thou hast given a banner to them that fear thee,
That it may be displayed because of the truth. Selah
⁵ That thy beloved may be delivered,
Save with thy right hand, and answer us.
⁶ God hath spoken in his holiness: I will exult;
I will divide Shechem, and mete out the valley of Succoth.
⁷ Gilead is mine, and Manasseh is mine;
Ephraim also is the defence of my head;
Judah is my sceptre.
⁸ Moab is my washpot;
Upon Edom will I cast my shoe:
Philistia, shout thou because of me.
⁹ Who will bring me into the strong city?
Who hath led me unto Edom?
¹⁰ Hast not thou, O God, cast us off?
And thou goest not forth, O God, with our hosts.
¹¹ Give us help against the adversary;
For vain is the help of man.
¹² Through God we shall do valiantly;
For he it is that will tread down our adversaries.

We used to blame God
For what went off the track
Floods fires massacres
Hurricanes
The plague

All meant to punish
Prostitutes no doubt
And homosexuals
And women who ended their pregnancies
That and people who burned down basilicas
And synagogues
Maybe because they could

After Einstein,
Multiple universities
Socrates
The Enlightenment
The New York Times
The Spoleto Festival

After we expanded our point of view
We realized that God
If there was a God
Read G-d
Read Yahweh
Did not exactly arrange for Auschwitz
Or cause Vesuvius to blow

Even Irish Catholics
Understood that Jesus Mary and Joseph
Were only exclamation points

Nevertheless
We still pray
To whomever we decide is God

Even though we do not know
And we know we do not know
We still ask him to destroy our enemies

We still entreat the Lord of Hosts
To save us from
Death
Addiction
And disease

And why is that?

We know

Do you?

Psalm Sixty-one

1 Hear my cry, O God;
Attend unto my prayer.
² From the end of the earth will I call unto thee,
When my heart is overwhelmed:
Lead me to the rock that is higher than I.
³ For thou hast been a refuge for me,
A strong tower from the enemy.
⁴ I will dwell in thy tabernacle for ever:
I will take refuge in the covert of thy wings. Selah
⁵ For thou, O God, hast heard my vows:
Thou hast given me the heritage of those that fear thy name.
⁶ Thou wilt prolong the king's life;
His years shall be as many generations.
⁷ He shall abide before God for ever:
Oh prepare loving kindness and truth, that they may preserve him.
⁸ So will I sing praise unto thy name for ever,
That I may daily perform my vows.

I've been run over by a semi-truck
Had a plate inserted in my head
Titanium
It anneals to bone
Hot cha!

My leg was amputated at the hip
Diabetes II
My eyesight's gone
My hearing's shot
My short-term memory—
Say what?

All my dogs, six mixed-breed
lie buried by the pond
Still, I pray unceasingly

To you
The ruler of my heart
Asking for forgiveness
For me
And for everyone I know

Even when I'm dead
And near dead
And blind
And losing what's left of my mind
I still will have my heart

More importantly

I will still have you

Psalm Sixty-two

1 My soul waiteth in silence for God only:
From him cometh my salvation.
² He only is my rock and my salvation:
He is my high tower; I shall not be greatly moved.
³ How long will ye set upon a man,
That ye may slay him, all of you,
Like a leaning wall, like a tottering fence?
⁴ They only consult to thrust him down from his dignity;
They delight in lies;
They bless with their mouth, but they curse inwardly. Selah
⁵ My soul, wait thou in silence for God only;
For my expectation is from him.
⁶ He only is my rock and my salvation:
He is my high tower; I shall not be moved.
⁷ With God is my salvation and my glory:
The rock of my strength, and my refuge, is in God.
⁸ Trust in him at all times, ye people;
Pour out your heart before him:
God is a refuge for us. Selah
⁹ Surely men of low degree are vanity, and men of high degree are a lie:
In the balances they will go up;
They are together lighter than vanity.
¹⁰ Trust not in oppression,
And become not vain in robbery:
If riches increase, set not your heart thereon.
¹¹ God hath spoken once,
Twice have I heard this,
That power belongeth unto God.
¹² Also unto thee, O Lord, belongeth loving kindness;
For thou renderest to every man according to his work.

I was beset with multiple bank accounts
Productive portfolios

Numerous homes
Staffs on hold
Squad cars circling
All
To keep me secure

Robbers came and stole my gold
Illness robbed me of my health
Old age my looks
Death most of my wives
And children

You are my rock and my salvation
I wait on you

In my inner core
That only you can see

I shall not be moved

Is that not true?

Tell me

Tell me now

Psalm Sixty-three

1 O God, thou art my God; earnestly will I seek thee:
My soul thirsteth for thee, my flesh longeth for thee,
In a dry and weary land, where no water is.
² So have I looked upon thee in the sanctuary,
To see thy power and thy glory.
³ Because thy loving kindness is better than life,
My lips shall praise thee.
⁴ So will I bless thee while I live:
I will lift up my hands in thy name.
⁵ My soul shall be satisfied as with marrow and fatness;
And my mouth shall praise thee with joyful lips;
⁶ When I remember thee upon my bed,
And meditate on thee in the night-watches.
⁷ For thou hast been my help,
And in the shadow of thy wings will I rejoice.
⁸ My soul followeth hard after thee:
Thy right hand upholdeth me.
⁹ But those that seek my soul, to destroy it,
Shall go into the lower parts of the earth.
¹⁰ They shall be given over to the power of the sword:
They shall be a portion for foxes.
¹¹ But the king shall rejoice in God:
Every one that sweareth by him shall glory;
For the mouth of them that speak lies shall be stopped.

I praise you
Not out of duty
Or obligation
But out of joy
And sometimes
Jubilation

I bring to you
The parade ground
Of my heart
The Mardi Gras within my soul

You are my light
My starry night
The source of life inside me

You are the journey after death
And the beginning of beauty

Whose majesty better to praise?
Whose perfection better to remember?

Those who seek to wreck my soul
Cannot touch
Your attendance within me

They cannot kill the love
I bear you

In their frustration
They can only wither in the winter cold
Seeking solace
With the wind

This is the world I have created

This is the dream I live

Psalm Sixty-four

1 Hear my voice, O God, in my complaint:
Preserve my life from fear of the enemy.
² Hide me from the secret counsel of evil-doers,
From the tumult of the workers of iniquity;
³ Who have whet their tongue like a sword,
And have aimed their arrows, even bitter words,
⁴ That they may shoot in secret places at the perfect:
Suddenly do they shoot at him, and fear not.
⁵ They encourage themselves in an evil purpose;
They commune of laying snares privily;
They say, Who will see them?
⁶ They search out iniquities;
We have accomplished, say they, a diligent search:
And the inward thought and the heart of every one is deep.
⁷ But God will shoot at them;
With an arrow suddenly shall they be wounded.
⁸ So they shall be made to stumble,
Their own tongue being against them:
All that see them shall wag the head.
⁹ And all men shall fear;
And they shall declare the work of God,
And shall wisely consider of his doing.
¹⁰ The righteous shall be glad in God, and shall take refuge in him;
And all the upright in heart shall glory.

Do you believe in justice
Where the wicked get their just desserts?

Or does justice only come in movies
Made before Hiroshima
The murders of the Kennedys
And Dr. King

Pictures with happy endings
Did I forget evictions
And hungry children
Women shot
Strangled
And beaten by husbands and lovers
And friends?

What do prisons say about the will of God?
Who are the guilty?
Who? said the owl
Not I, said the fox

All men shall declare the work of God they say
The righteous shall trust in the Lord

That depends on the studio
The investors
And the script

Psalm Sixty-five

1 Praise waiteth for thee, O God, in Zion;
And unto thee shall the vow be performed.
² O thou that hearest prayer,
Unto thee shall all flesh come.
³ Iniquities prevail against me:
As for our transgressions, thou wilt forgive them.
⁴ Blessed is the man whom thou choosest,
And causest to approach unto thee,
That he may dwell in thy courts:
We shall be satisfied with the goodness of thy house,
Thy holy temple.
⁵ By terrible things thou wilt answer us in righteousness,
O God of our salvation,
Thou that art the confidence of all the ends of the earth,
And of them that are afar off upon the sea:
⁶ Who by his strength setteth fast the mountains,
Being girded about with might;
⁷ Who stilleth the roaring of the seas,
The roaring of their waves,
And the tumult of the peoples.
⁸ They also that dwell in the uttermost parts are afraid at thy tokens:
Thou makest the outgoings of the morning and evening to rejoice.
⁹ Thou visitest the earth, and waterest it,
Thou greatly enrichest it;
The river of God is full of water:
Thou providest them grain, when thou hast so prepared the earth.
¹⁰ Thou waterest its furrows abundantly;
Thou settlest the ridges thereof:
Thou makest it soft with showers;
Thou blessest the springing thereof.
¹¹ Thou crownest the year with thy goodness;
And thy paths drop fatness.
¹² They drop upon the pastures of the wilderness;

And the hills are girded with joy.
¹³ The pastures are clothed with flocks;
The valleys also are covered over with grain;
They shout for joy, they also sing.

Have you noticed
We seem to be waiting on God
Or gods?
Something wonderful
We can count on

In the telling
They control the seas
The bounty of the land
And maybe the course of the human heart
Ah so

According to the Psalm
They setteth fast the mountains
And bless the valleys

When no one's looking
They provide pastures
And all good things to eat

All of which
Get this
When things go wrong
Especially drought
Famine
And forest fires
Give way
To rain dances
Imprecations
Promises
Oaths
Anything

And eventually to
Sacrificing animals

And when all else fails
To cutting out the hearts
Of boys and girls

Then, when sacrifice goes out of style
We build cathedrals
And preach to the unsanctified

All praise and glory to
To scientists
Inventors
And technologists
Tesla
Edison
Jonas Salk

They spend their lives
Addressing
Anything but gods

Psalm Sixty-six

1 Make a joyful noise unto God, all the earth:
² Sing forth the glory of his name:
Make his praise glorious.
³ Say unto God, How terrible are thy works!
Through the greatness of thy power
Shall thine enemies submit themselves unto thee.
⁴ All the earth shall worship thee,
And shall sing unto thee;
They shall sing to thy name.
⁵ Come, and see the works of God;
He is terrible in his doing toward the children of men.
⁶ He turned the sea into dry land;
They went through the river on foot:
There did we rejoice in him.
⁷ He ruleth by his might for ever;
His eyes observe the nations:
Let not the rebellious exalt themselves.
⁸ Oh bless our God, ye peoples,
And make the voice of his praise to be heard;
⁹ Who holdeth our soul in life,
And suffereth not our feet to be moved.
¹⁰ For thou, O God, hast proved us:
Thou hast tried us, as silver is tried.
¹¹ Thou broughtest us into the net;
Thou layedst a sore burden upon our loins.
¹² Thou didst cause men to ride over our heads;
We went through fire and through water;
But thou broughtest us out into a wealthy place.
¹³ I will come into thy house with burnt-offerings;
I will pay thee my vows,
¹⁴ Which my lips uttered,
And my mouth spake, when I was in distress.
¹⁵ I will offer unto thee burnt-offerings of fatlings,

With the incense of rams;
I will offer bullocks with goats.
¹⁶ Come, and hear, all ye that fear God,
And I will declare what he hath done for my soul.
¹⁷ I cried unto him with my mouth,
And he was extolled with my tongue.
¹⁸ If I regard iniquity in my heart,
The Lord will not hear:
¹⁹ But verily God hath heard;
He hath attended to the voice of my prayer.
²⁰ Blessed be God,
Who hath not turned away my prayer,
Nor his loving kindness from me.

Why are we tested?
Or is our suffering
A matter of matter half-evolved?

Still learning
Still looking at the sun
As if light will reveal
What we think
We need to know

Plowing through tomes
In ancient libraries
Deciphering wisdom written in code
On parchment burned by fundamentalists

Is the knowledge we keep searching for
More a matter of the love
We cannot find
In opioids
Mint julips
Multiple marriages
And philanthropy?

Make a joyful noise all ye lands
The Psalmist says
We will bring burnt offerings
And praise his holy name

Sure

Too little too late
Said the psychic to the priest

Psalm Sixty-seven

1 God be merciful unto us, and bless us,
And cause his face to shine upon us; Selah
² That thy way may be known upon earth,
Thy salvation among all nations.
³ Let the peoples praise thee, O God;
Let all the peoples praise thee.
⁴ Oh let the nations be glad and sing for joy;
For thou wilt judge the peoples with equity,
And govern the nations upon earth. Selah
⁵ Let the peoples praise thee, O God;
Let all the peoples praise thee.
⁶ The earth hath yielded its increase:
God, even our own God, will bless us.
⁷ God will bless us;
And all the ends of the earth shall fear him.

We need someone to be merciful to us,
God knows

Don't we?

We need blessings too

And health

Praise
To the God
Who hides his face
His gender
His body
Parenthetically
Her body too
Unless that body would be us

Layers upon layers
Of mind and heart
Such is our destiny

What do you think?

Psalm Sixty-eight

1 Let God arise, let his enemies be scattered;
Let them also that hate him flee before him.
² As smoke is driven away, so drive them away:
As wax melteth before the fire,
So let the wicked perish at the presence of God.
³ But let the righteous be glad; let them exult before God:
Yea, let them rejoice with gladness.
⁴ Sing unto God, sing praises to his name:
Cast up a highway for him that rideth through the deserts;
His name is God; and exult ye before him.
⁵ A father of the fatherless, and a judge of the widows,
Is God in his holy habitation.
⁶ God setteth the solitary in families:
He bringeth out the prisoners into prosperity;
But the rebellious dwell in a parched land.
⁷ O God, when thou wentest forth before thy people,
When thou didst march through the wilderness; Selah
⁸ The earth trembled,
The heavens also dropped rain at the presence of God:
Yon Sinai trembled at the presence of God, the God of Israel.
⁹ Thou, O God, didst send a plentiful rain,
Thou didst confirm thine inheritance, when it was weary.
¹⁰ Thy congregation dwelt therein:
Thou, O God, didst prepare of thy goodness for the poor.
¹¹ The Lord giveth the word:
The women that publish the tidings are a great host.
¹² Kings of armies flee, they flee;
And she that tarrieth at home divideth the spoil.
¹³ When ye lie among the sheepfolds,
It is as the wings of a dove covered with silver,
And her pinions with yellow gold.
¹⁴ When the Almighty scattered kings therein,
It was as when it snoweth in Zalmon.

¹⁵ *A mountain of God is the mountain of Bashan;*
A high mountain is the mountain of Bashan.
¹⁶ *Why look ye askance, ye high mountains,*
At the mountain which God hath desired for his abode?
Yea, God will dwell in it for ever.
¹⁷ *The chariots of God are twenty thousand,*
Even thousands upon thousands:
The Lord is among them, as in Sinai, in the sanctuary.
¹⁸ *Thou hast ascended on high, thou hast led away captives;*
Thou hast received gifts among men,
Yea, among the rebellious also, that God God might dwell with them.
¹⁹ *Blessed be the Lord, who daily beareth our burden,*
Even the God who is our salvation. Selah
²⁰ *God is unto us a God of deliverances;*
And unto God the Lord belongeth escape from death.
²¹ *But God will smite through the head of his enemies,*
The hairy scalp of such a one as goeth on still in his guiltiness.
²² *The Lord said, I will bring again from Bashan,*
I will bring them again from the depths of the sea;
²³ *That thou mayest crush them, dipping thy foot in blood,*
That the tongue of thy dogs may have its portion from thine enemies.
²⁴ *They have seen thy goings, O God,*
Even the goings of my God, my King, into the sanctuary.
²⁵ *The singers went before, the minstrels followed after,*
In the midst of the damsels playing with timbrels.
²⁶ *Bless ye God in the congregations,*
Even the Lord, ye that are of the fountain of Israel.
²⁷ *There is little Benjamin their ruler,*
The princes of Judah and their council,
The princes of Zebulun, the princes of Naphtali.
²⁸ *Thy God hath commanded thy strength:*
Strengthen, O God, that which thou hast wrought for us.
²⁹ *Because of thy temple at Jerusalem*
Kings shall bring presents unto thee.
³⁰ *Rebuke the wild beast of the reeds,*

The multitude of the bulls, with the calves of the peoples,
Trampling under foot the pieces of silver:
He hath scattered the peoples that delight in war.
³¹ Princes shall come out of Egypt;
Ethiopia shall haste to stretch out her hands unto God.
³² Sing unto God, ye kingdoms of the earth;
Oh sing praises unto the Lord; Selah
³³ To him that rideth upon the heaven of heavens, which are of old;
Lo, he uttereth his voice, a mighty voice.
³⁴ Ascribe ye strength unto God:
His excellency is over Israel,
And his strength is in the skies.
³⁵ O God, thou art terrible out of thy holy places:
The God of Israel, he giveth strength and power unto his people.
Blessed be God.

I can't wait
For my foot to be dipped
In the blood of my enemies
And the tongue of my dog in the same

So proclaims the Psalm

This is our God
Apparently

The earth shakes
The heavens drop
At the sight of Him

Wow
The Almighty scatters kings
They say
That must have been World War One
Two
And counting

The chariots of God are twenty thousand
Says the psalm
They must refer to tanks and armored vehicles

And the biggest bombs in the universe.

Once again
God is on our side

He giveth strength
And power
Unto his people

It's us and them
The people of God
And the wicked

God will subdue them in our sight

That's why we made him God

Good job

Psalm Sixty-nine

1 Save me, O God;
For the waters are come in unto my soul.
² I sink in deep mire, where there is no standing:
I am come into deep waters, where the floods overflow me.
³ I am weary with my crying; my throat is dried:
Mine eyes fail while I wait for my God.
⁴ They that hate me without a cause
Are more than the hairs of my head:
They that would cut me off,
Being mine enemies wrongfully, are mighty:
That which I took not away I have to restore.
⁵ O God, thou knowest my foolishness;
And my sins are not hid from thee.
⁶ Let not them that wait for thee be put to shame through me,
O Lord God of hosts:
Let not those that seek thee be brought to dishonor through me,
O God of Israel.
⁷ Because for thy sake I have borne reproach;
Shame hath covered my face.
⁸ I am become a stranger unto my brethren,
And an alien unto my mother's children.
⁹ For the zeal of thy house hath eaten me up;
And the reproaches of them that reproach thee are fallen upon me.
¹⁰ When I wept, and chastened my soul with fasting,
That was to my reproach.
¹¹ When I made sackcloth my clothing,
I became a byword unto them.
¹² They that sit in the gate talk of me;
And I am the song of the drunkards.
¹³ But as for me, my prayer is unto thee, O God, in an acceptable time:
O God, in the abundance of thy loving kindness,
Answer me in the truth of thy salvation.
¹⁴ Deliver me out of the mire, and let me not sink:

Let me be delivered from them that hate me,
And out of the deep waters.
15 Let not the waterflood overwhelm me,
Neither let the deep swallow me up;
And let not the pit shut its mouth upon me.
16 Answer me, O God; for thy loving kindness is good:
According to the multitude of thy tender mercies turn thou unto me.
17 And hide not thy face from thy servant;
For I am in distress; answer me speedily.
18 Draw nigh unto my soul, and redeem it:
Ransom me because of mine enemies.
19 Thou knowest my reproach, and my shame, and my dishonor:
Mine adversaries are all before thee.
20 Reproach hath broken my heart; and I am full of heaviness:
And I looked for some to take pity, but there was none;
And for comforters, but I found none.
21 They gave me also gall for my food;
And in my thirst they gave me vinegar to drink.
22 Let their table before them become a snare;
And when they are in peace, let it become a trap.
23 Let their eyes be darkened, so that they cannot see;
And make their loins continually to shake.
24 Pour out thine indignation upon them,
And let the fierceness of thine anger overtake them.
25 Let their habitation be desolate;
Let none dwell in their tents.
26 For they persecute him whom thou hast smitten;
And they tell of the sorrow of those whom thou hast wounded.
27 Add iniquity unto their iniquity;
And let them not come into thy righteousness.
28 Let them be blotted out of the book of life,
And not be written with the righteous.
29 But I am poor and sorrowful:
Let thy salvation, O God, set me up on high.
30 I will praise the name of God with a song,
And will magnify him with thanksgiving.

³¹ *And it will please God better than an ox,*
Or a bullock that hath horns and hoofs.
³² *The meek have seen it, and are glad:*
Ye that seek after God, let your heart live.
³³ *For God heareth the needy,*
And despiseth not his prisoners.
³⁴ *Let heaven and earth praise him,*
The seas, and everything that moveth therein.
³⁵ *For God will save Zion, and build the cities of Judah;*
And they shall abide there, and have it in possession.
³⁶ *The seed also of his servants shall inherit it;*
And they that love his name shall dwell therein.

I need a god to take revenge on me
Where are you now?

I have been slandered
And whispered about
Subjected to lies
My people starved
Robbed
Our women raped
Our children abandoned

We have fought back
With rage
And murder at every turn
An eye for an eye
A tooth for a tooth
Isn't that the way?

With no sense of gratitude
For even songbirds
Or the gentle breeze

I lie at the bottom of the sea
The waters pressing on my soul

Lord do not let me disappear
Do not hide your face from me

Rescue me
And teach me how to love

Whoever you are

Psalm Seventy

1 Make haste, O God, to deliver me;
Make haste to help me, O God.
² Let them be put to shame and confounded
That seek after my soul:
Let them be turned backward and brought to dishonor
That delight in my hurt.
³ Let them be turned back by reason of their shame
That say, Aha, aha.
⁴ Let all those that seek thee rejoice and be glad in thee;
And let such as love thy salvation say continually,
Let God be magnified.
⁵ But I am poor and needy;
Make haste unto me, O God:
Thou art my help and my deliverer;
O God, make no tarrying.

I pray for those who seek the light

I celebrate souls who know
They belong to the Earth
And in their belonging
Embrace everyone alive

I praise those
Who discover beauty everywhere
Even in hurricanes
Who overrule the dark
Who offer their hand to strangers
To children
To those in distress

I am poor
I am needy
I am waiting to be filled

What is this power of mine
I keep hearing about?

Hurry to me O God
Whoever you may be

Hurry soon

Psalm Seventy-one

1 In thee, O God, do I take refuge:
Let me never be put to shame.
² Deliver me in thy righteousness, and rescue me:
Bow down thine ear unto me, and save me.
³ Be thou to me a rock of habitation,
Whereunto I may continually resort:
Thou hast given commandment to save me;
For thou art my rock and my fortress.
⁴ Rescue me, O my God, out of the hand of the wicked,
Out of the hand of the unrighteous and cruel man.
⁵ For thou art my hope, O Lord God:
Thou art my trust from my youth.
⁶ By thee have I been holden up from the womb;
Thou art he that took me out of my mother's bowels:
My praise shall be continually of thee.
⁷ I am as a wonder unto many;
But thou art my strong refuge.
⁸ My mouth shall be filled with thy praise,
And with thy honor all the day.
⁹ Cast me not off in the time of old age;
Forsake me not when my strength faileth.
¹⁰ For mine enemies speak concerning me;
And they that watch for my soul take counsel together,
¹¹ Saying, God hath forsaken him:
Pursue and take him; for there is none to deliver.
¹² O God, be not far from me;
O my God, make haste to help me.
¹³ Let them be put to shame and consumed
That are adversaries to my soul;
Let them be covered with reproach and dishonor that seek my hurt.
¹⁴ But I will hope continually,
And will praise thee yet more and more.
¹⁵ My mouth shall tell of thy righteousness,

And of thy salvation all the day;
For I know not the numbers thereof.
[16] *I will come with the mighty acts of the LORD God:*
I will make mention of thy righteousness, even of thine only.
[17] *O God, thou hast taught me from my youth;*
And hitherto have I declared thy wondrous works.
[18] *Yea, even when I am old and grayheaded, O God, forsake me not,*
Until I have declared thy strength unto the next generation,
Thy might to every one that is to come.
[19] *Thy righteousness also, O God, is very high;*
Thou who hast done great things, O God, who is like unto thee?
[20] *Thou, who hast showed us many and sore troubles,*
Wilt quicken us again,
And wilt bring us up again from the depths of the earth.
[21] *Increase thou my greatness,*
And turn again and comfort me.
[22] *I will also praise thee with the psaltery,*
Even thy truth, O my God:
Unto thee will I sing praises with the harp,
O thou Holy One of Israel.
[23] *My lips shall shout for joy when I sing praises unto thee;*
And my soul, which thou hast redeemed.
[24] *My tongue also shall talk of thy righteousness all the day long;*
For they are put to shame, for they are confounded, that seek my hurt.

Let us pray for clear minds
And plain thinking

Perfect strategy in all our plans

Let us hope
To steer clear of cruelty
And people who wound

Let us learn to trust
Each other
In spite of scams
And grifters
And fabulous fortune finders
From New York City
And Nigeria

Have I got a deal?
No, not that
Only the powers of Gaia
And the glory of get up and go
Isn't that enough for now?

When we are old and weak
And nodding by the swimming pool
Let us wait for deliverance

You will lift us up from the depths of the earth
From the dark night of depression
You will comfort us on every side.

And my soul shall be redeemed

Psalm Seventy-two

1 Give the king thy judgments, O God,
And thy righteousness unto the king's son.
² He will judge thy people with righteousness,
And thy poor with justice.
³ The mountains shall bring peace to the people,
And the hills, in righteousness.
⁴ He will judge the poor of the people,
He will save the children of the needy,
And will break in pieces the oppressor.
⁵ They shall fear thee while the sun endureth,
And so long as the moon, throughout all generations.
⁶ He will come down like rain upon the mown grass,
As showers that water the earth.
⁷ In his days shall the righteous flourish,
And abundance of peace, till the moon be no more.
⁸ He shall have dominion also from sea to sea,
And from the River unto the ends of the earth.
⁹ They that dwell in the wilderness shall bow before him;
And his enemies shall lick the dust.
¹⁰ The kings of Tarshish and of the isles shall render tribute:
The kings of Sheba and Seba shall offer gifts.
¹¹ Yea, all kings shall fall down before him;
All nations shall serve him.
¹² For he will deliver the needy when he crieth,
And the poor, that hath no helper.
¹³ He will have pity on the poor and needy,
And the souls of the needy he will save.
¹⁴ He will redeem their soul from oppression and violence;
And precious will their blood be in his sight:
¹⁵ And they shall live; and to him shall be given of the gold of Sheba:
And men shall pray for him continually;
They shall bless him all the day long.
¹⁶ There shall be abundance of grain in the earth

Upon the top of the mountains;
The fruit thereof shall shake like Lebanon:
And they of the city shall flourish like grass of the earth.
[17] *His name shall endure for ever;*
His name shall be continued as long as the sun:
And men shall be blessed in him;
All nations shall call him happy.
[18] *Blessed be God God, the God of Israel,*
Who only doeth wondrous things:
[19] *And blessed be his glorious name for ever;*
And let the whole earth be filled with his glory.
Amen, and Amen.
[20] *The prayers of David the son of Jesse are ended.*

Who judges then
The oppressors of the poor?

Who decides the punishment
For those who injure children
And the innocent?

When will the righteous flourish?
When will we have peace
For as long as the moon endures
And the sun maintains its ancient place?

When will the cities grow like grass?

Where is the God who has disappeared
From our sight
And from the hearts of the multitudes?

We pray for peace
While we build weapons
And celebrate wars and warriors
And battle cries

What hope for us?
After two hundred and fifty million years
Still barbarians
Still Philistines
Still boors

Blessed be the Lord God, who doeth only wondrous things.
And still we are empty inside

Blessed be his glorious name for ever

And blessed be us, caught in unknowing
Transfixed by the beauty of the earth
Our brains on fire
Our hearts torn asunder

Yes, blessed be us

Waiting for deliverance

Psalm Seventy-three

¹ *Surely God is good to Israel,*
Even to such as are pure in heart.
² *But as for me, my feet were almost gone;*
My steps had well nigh slipped.
³ *For I was envious at the arrogant,*
When I saw the prosperity of the wicked.
⁴ *For there are no pangs in their death;*
But their strength is firm.
⁵ *They are not in trouble as other men;*
Neither are they plagued like other men.
⁶ *Therefore pride is as a chain about their neck;*
Violence covereth them as a garment.
⁷ *Their eyes stand out with fatness:*
They have more than heart could wish.
⁸ *They scoff, and in wickedness utter oppression:*
They speak loftily.
⁹ *They have set their mouth in the heavens,*
And their tongue walketh through the earth.
¹⁰ *Therefore his people return hither:*
And waters of a full cup are drained by them.
¹¹ *And they say, How doth God know?*
And is there knowledge in the Most High?
¹² *Behold, these are the wicked;*
And, being alway at ease, they increase in riches.
¹³ *Surely in vain have I cleansed my heart,*
And washed my hands in innocency;
¹⁴ *For all the day long have I been plagued,*
And chastened every morning.
¹⁵ *If I had said, I will speak thus;*
Behold, I had dealt treacherously with the generation of thy children.
¹⁶ *When I thought how I might know this,*
It was too painful for me;
¹⁷ *Until I went into the sanctuary of God,*

And considered their latter end.
¹⁸ Surely thou settest them in slippery places:
Thou castest them down to destruction.
¹⁹ How are they become a desolation in a moment!
They are utterly consumed with terrors.
²⁰ As a dream when one awaketh,
So, O Lord, when thou awakest, thou wilt despise their image.
²¹ For my soul was grieved,
And I was pricked in my heart:
²² So brutish was I, and ignorant;
I was as a beast before thee.
²³ Nevertheless I am continually with thee:
Thou hast holden my right hand.
²⁴ Thou wilt guide me with thy counsel,
And afterward receive me to glory.
²⁵ Whom have I in heaven but thee?
And there is none upon earth that I desire besides thee.
²⁶ My flesh and my heart faileth;
But God is the strength of my heart and my portion for ever.
²⁷ For, lo, they that are far from thee shall perish:
Thou hast destroyed all them that play the harlot, departing from thee.
²⁸ But it is good for me to draw near unto God:
I have made the Lord God my refuge,
That I may tell of all thy works.

Some people make money easily
Piece 'o cake
Accumulating cars and real estate
Infinity pools
Hi-tech tools
Husbands
Trophy wives
And plastic surgery

Their increasing portfolio
Allows them
Extravagance at every turn

Am I jealous?
Yes
Envious?
Of course

I want my private plane
My Lamborghini
My best friends to be movie stars
Why not?

Question:
Why does the well-heeled
Establishment

Need armies
Intercontinental ballistic missiles
And nuclear bombs
To feel assured?
Why do they need to own political campaigns?

Am I shaming the wealthy
Making them scapegoats
Blaming them for poverty
And prisons?

Is this mere rhetoric?

Possibly
Yes
Of course
Sans doubt

Have I been brainwashed?
Probably yes

Where is the poetry?
The quarrel within myself

The poor also
Turn this world
Into black and white

Raging
Polarizing
Categorizing
Catastrophe

I claim to be one with God
God the strength of my heart
I say
Some days
I like to imagine God abhors the rich

When in fact
He adores them too

Assuming he exists

At least
That's the hypothesis
Prosperity gospel
Dontcha know?

So far, God has not weighed in

Psalm Seventy-four

1 O God, why hast thou cast us off for ever?
Why doth thine anger smoke against the sheep of thy pasture?
² Remember thy congregation, which thou hast gotten of old,
Which thou hast redeemed to be the tribe of thine inheritance;
And mount Zion, wherein thou hast dwelt.
³ Lift up thy feet unto the perpetual ruins,
All the evil that the enemy hath done in the sanctuary.
⁴ Thine adversaries have roared in the midst of thine assembly;
They have set up their ensigns for signs.
⁵ They seemed as men that lifted up
Axes upon a thicket of trees.
⁶ And now all the carved work thereof
They break down with hatchet and hammers.
⁷ They have set thy sanctuary on fire;
They have profaned the dwelling-place of thy name
By casting it to the ground.
⁸ They said in their heart, Let us make havoc of them altogether:
They have burned up all the synagogues of God in the land.
⁹ We see not our signs:
There is no more any prophet;
Neither is there among us any that knoweth how long.
¹⁰ How long, O God, shall the adversary reproach?
Shall the enemy blaspheme thy name for ever?
¹¹ Why drawest thou back thy hand, even thy right hand?
Pluck it out of thy bosom and consume them.
¹² Yet God is my King of old,
Working salvation in the midst of the earth.
¹³ Thou didst divide the sea by thy strength:
Thou brakest the heads of the sea-monsters in the waters.
¹⁴ Thou brakest the heads of leviathan in pieces;
Thou gavest him to be food to the people inhabiting the wilderness.
¹⁵ Thou didst cleave fountain and flood:
Thou driedst up mighty rivers.

¹⁶ *The day is thine, the night also is thine:*
Thou hast prepared the light and the sun.
¹⁷ *Thou hast set all the borders of the earth:*
Thou hast made summer and winter.
¹⁸ *Remember this, that the enemy hath reproached, O God,*
And that a foolish people hath blasphemed thy name.
¹⁹ *Oh deliver not the soul of thy turtle-dove unto the wild beast:*
Forget not the life of thy poor for ever.
²⁰ *Have respect unto the covenant;*
For the dark places of the earth are full of the habitations of violence.
²¹ *Oh let not the oppressed return ashamed:*
Let the poor and needy praise thy name.
²² *Arise, O God, plead thine own cause:*
Remember how the foolish man reproacheth thee all the day.
²³ *Forget not the voice of thine adversaries:*
The tumult of those that rise up against thee ascendeth continually.

What do we do with the Nazis among us?

Even now
Look around
Evocations of a master race
In proud supremacy
White-eyed rage
Burning synagogues
And mosques
Even building walls

What do we do with fundamentalists?
Destroying images
Of unknown gods
Obliterating the cries of girls
Stoning adulterers
Assassinating homosexuals
Anything to circumvent the dark

Which god do we choose?
Or none?
Maybe something imagined
Something new and wonderful

Who hast prepared the sun?
Who has made summer and winter
And taught the sparrows
The mere suggestions of symphony?

Or did it happen by itself?

The dark places of the earth are full of the habitations of cruelty,
Proclaims the Psalm

As the storm troopers stand around
We drown in our madness
Waiting for a better god

Let him step forth and we will worship him

Hello?

Psalm Seventy-five

1 We give thanks unto thee, O God;
We give thanks, for thy name is near:
Men tell of thy wondrous works.
² When I shall find the set time, I will judge uprightly.
³ The earth and all the inhabitants thereof are dissolved:
I have set up the pillars of it. Selah
⁴ I said unto the arrogant, Deal not arrogantly;
And to the wicked, Lift not up the horn:
⁵ Lift not up your horn on high;
Speak not with a stiff neck.
⁶ For neither from the east, nor from the west,
Nor yet from the south, cometh lifting up.
⁷ But God is the judge:
He putteth down one, and lifteth up another.
⁸ For in the hand of God there is a cup, and the wine foameth;
It is full of mixture, and he poureth out of the same:
Surely the dregs thereof, all the wicked of the earth shall drain them,
and drink them.
⁹ But I will declare for ever,
I will sing praises to the God of Jacob.
¹⁰ All the horns of the wicked also will I cut off;
But the horns of the righteous shall be lifted up.

We begin and end the day
With gratitude
For the spirit that rides the winds
And brightens the firmament

We live with thanksgiving
For this wondrous place
We call home
Forgetting
The darkness that would envelop us

And all our surrounding enemies
If for a moment we forgot who we are
And why we are here

In all things
We praise the light
And give thanks for you
Now and forever

Amen

Psalm Seventy-six

1 In Judah is God known:
His name is great in Israel.
² In Salem also is his tabernacle,
And his dwelling-place in Zion.
³ There he brake the arrows of the bow;
The shield, and the sword, and the battle. Selah
⁴ Glorious art thou and excellent,
From the mountains of prey.
⁵ The stouthearted are made a spoil,
They have slept their sleep;
And none of the men of might have found their hands.
⁶ At thy rebuke, O God of Jacob,
Both chariot and horse are cast into a dead sleep.
⁷ Thou, even thou, art to be feared;
And who may stand in thy sight when once thou art angry?
⁸ Thou didst cause sentence to be heard from heaven;
The earth feared, and was still,
⁹ When God arose to judgment,
To save all the meek of the earth. Selah
¹⁰ Surely the wrath of man shall praise thee:
The residue of wrath shalt thou gird upon thee.
¹¹ Vow, and pay unto God your God:
Let all that are round about him bring presents
Unto him that ought to be feared.
¹² He will cut off the spirit of princes:
He is terrible to the kings of the earth.

On this earth
We know our goddess well
In the seasons
We see the beauty of her mind
In the fruits of the fields
We know her heart

We are the children of Gaia
She embraces us
When we care for her

When we protect her
She does not fail us

In her there is no wrath
No punishment

Only the power of her breath
The force of her dance

Her excitement in being alive

Psalm Seventy-seven

1 I will cry unto God with my voice,
Even unto God with my voice; and he will give ear unto me.
² In the day of my trouble I sought the Lord:
My hand was stretched out in the night, and slacked not;
My soul refused to be comforted.
³ I remember God, and am disquieted:
I complain, and my spirit is overwhelmed. Selah
⁴ Thou holdest mine eyes watching:
I am so troubled that I cannot speak.
⁵ I have considered the days of old,
The years of ancient times.
⁶ I call to remembrance my song in the night:
I commune with mine own heart;
And my spirit maketh diligent search.
⁷ Will the Lord cast off for ever?
And will he be favorable no more?
⁸ Is his loving kindness clean gone for ever?
Doth his promise fail for evermore?
⁹ Hath God forgotten to be gracious?
Hath he in anger shut up his tender mercies? Selah
¹⁰ And I said, This is my infirmity;
But I will remember the years of the right hand of the Most High.
¹¹ I will make mention of the deeds of God;
For I will remember thy wonders of old.
¹² I will meditate also upon all thy work,
And muse on thy doings.
¹³ Thy way, O God, is in the sanctuary:
Who is a great god like unto God?
¹⁴ Thou art the God that doest wonders:
Thou hast made known thy strength among the peoples.
¹⁵ Thou hast with thine arm redeemed thy people,
The sons of Jacob and Joseph. Selah
¹⁶ The waters saw thee, O God;

The waters saw thee, they were afraid:
The depths also trembled.
[17] The clouds poured out water;
The skies sent out a sound:
Thine arrows also went abroad.
[18] The voice of thy thunder was in the whirlwind;
The lightnings lightened the world:
The earth trembled and shook.
[19] Thy way was in the sea,
And thy paths in the great waters,
And thy footsteps were not known.
[20] Thou leddest thy people like a flock,
By the hand of Moses and Aaron.

Our anointed leaders sell their souls for coin
Their wickedness infects the air
While we breathe unhappiness and pain

Have you forgotten us?

Remember
When we lighted candles to the Lord
And asked you to look out for us

Now I lay me down to sleep
And pray the Lord my soul to keep
Never forget us
Especially in the dark

We were surrounded once again
By concentration camps
And genocide
Your people transported into the flames

And where were you?

Where are you now?

When the course of evil flows again
When oceans die
And waters turn to blood

Once
When you spoke
Thunder boomed
The earth trembled
You vanquished your enemies

Now your voice is silent
Your footsteps are no longer known
Your enemies grow closer
And we remain alone

Listening

Psalm Seventy-eight

1 Give ear, O my people, to my law:
Incline your ears to the words of my mouth.
² I will open my mouth in a parable;
I will utter dark sayings of old,
³ Which we have heard and known,
And our fathers have told us.
⁴ We will not hide them from their children,
Telling to the generation to come the praises of God,
And his strength, and his wondrous works that he hath done.
⁵ For he established a testimony in Jacob,
And appointed a law in Israel,
Which he commanded our fathers,
That they should make them known to their children;
⁶ That the generation to come might know them,
Even the children that should be born;
Who should arise and tell them to their children,
⁷ That they might set their hope in God,
And not forget the works of God,
But keep his commandments,
⁸ And might not be as their fathers,
A stubborn and rebellious generation,
A generation that set not their heart aright,
And whose spirit was not stedfast with God.
⁹ The children of Ephraim, being armed and carrying bows,
Turned back in the day of battle.
¹⁰ They kept not the covenant of God,
And refused to walk in his law;
¹¹ And they forgat his doings,
And his wondrous works that he had showed them.
¹² Marvellous things did he in the sight of their fathers,
In the land of Egypt, in the field of Zoan.
¹³ He clave the sea, and caused them to pass through;
And he made the waters to stand as a heap.

^{14} *In the day-time also he led them with a cloud,*
And all the night with a light of fire.
^{15} *He clave rocks in the wilderness,*
And gave them drink abundantly as out of the depths.
^{16} *He brought streams also out of the rock,*
And caused waters to run down like rivers.
^{17} *Yet went they on still to sin against him,*
To rebel against the Most High in the desert.
^{18} *And they tempted God in their heart*
By asking food according to their desire.
^{19} *Yea, they spake against God;*
They said, Can God prepare a table in the wilderness?
^{20} *Behold, he smote the rock, so that waters gushed out,*
And streams overflowed;
Can he give bread also?
Will he provide flesh for his people?
^{21} *Therefore God heard, and was wroth;*
And a fire was kindled against Jacob,
And anger also went up against Israel;
^{22} *Because they believed not in God,*
And trusted not in his salvation.
^{23} *Yet he commanded the skies above,*
And opened the doors of heaven;
^{24} *And he rained down manna upon them to eat,*
And gave them food from heaven.
^{25} *Man did eat the bread of the mighty:*
He sent them food to the full.
^{26} *He caused the east wind to blow in the heavens;*
And by his power he guided the south wind.
^{27} *He rained flesh also upon them as the dust,*
And winged birds as the sand of the seas:
^{28} *And he let it fall in the midst of their camp,*
Round about their habitations.
^{29} *So they did eat, and were well filled;*
And he gave them their own desire.

³⁰ They were not estranged from that which they desired,
Their food was yet in their mouths,
³¹ When the anger of God went up against them,
And slew of the fattest of them,
And smote down the young men of Israel.
³² For all this they sinned still,
And believed not in his wondrous works.
³³ Therefore their days did he consume in vanity,
And their years in terror.
³⁴ When he slew them, then they inquired after him;
And they returned and sought God earnestly.
³⁵ And they remembered that God was their rock,
And the Most High God their redeemer.
³⁶ But they flattered him with their mouth,
And lied unto him with their tongue.
³⁷ For their heart was not right with him,
Neither were they faithful in his covenant.
³⁸ But he, being merciful, forgave their iniquity,
And destroyed them not:
Yea, many a time turned he his anger away,
And did not stir up all his wrath.
³⁹ And he remembered that they were but flesh,
A wind that passeth away, and cometh not again.
⁴⁰ How oft did they rebel against him in the wilderness,
And grieve him in the desert!
⁴¹ And they turned again and tempted God,
And provoked the Holy One of Israel.
⁴² They remembered not his hand,
Nor the day when he redeemed them from the adversary;
⁴³ How he set his signs in Egypt,
And his wonders in the field of Zoan,
⁴⁴ And turned their rivers into blood,
And their streams, so that they could not drink.
⁴⁵ He sent among them swarms of flies, which devoured them;
And frogs, which destroyed them.

⁴⁶ He gave also their increase unto the caterpillar,
And their labor unto the locust.
⁴⁷ He destroyed their vines with hail,
And their sycomore-trees with frost.
⁴⁸ He gave over their cattle also to the hail,
And their flocks to hot thunderbolts.
⁴⁹ He cast upon them the fierceness of his anger,
Wrath, and indignation, and trouble,
A band of angels of evil.
⁵⁰ He made a path for his anger;
He spared not their soul from death,
But gave their life over to the pestilence,
⁵¹ And smote all the first-born in Egypt,
The chief of their strength in the tents of Ham.
⁵² But he led forth his own people like sheep,
And guided them in the wilderness like a flock.
⁵³ And he led them safely, so that they feared not;
But the sea overwhelmed their enemies.
⁵⁴ And he brought them to the border of his sanctuary,
To this mountain, which his right hand had gotten.
⁵⁵ He drove out the nations also before them,
And allotted them for an inheritance by line,
And made the tribes of Israel to dwell in their tents.
⁵⁶ Yet they tempted and rebelled against the Most High God,
And kept not his testimonies;
⁵⁷ But turned back, and dealt treacherously like their fathers:
They were turned aside like a deceitful bow.
⁵⁸ For they provoked him to anger with their high places,
And moved him to jealousy with their graven images.
⁵⁹ When God heard this, he was wroth,
And greatly abhorred Israel;
⁶⁰ So that he forsook the tabernacle of Shiloh,
The tent which he placed among men;
⁶¹ And delivered his strength into captivity,
And his glory into the adversary's hand.

⁶² *He gave his people over also unto the sword,*
And was wroth with his inheritance.
⁶³ *Fire devoured their young men;*
And their virgins had no marriage-song.
⁶⁴ *Their priests fell by the sword;*
And their widows made no lamentation.
⁶⁵ *Then the Lord awaked as one out of sleep,*
Like a mighty man that shouteth by reason of wine.
⁶⁶ *And he smote his adversaries backward:*
He put them to a perpetual reproach.
⁶⁷ *Moreover he refused the tent of Joseph,*
And chose not the tribe of Ephraim,
⁶⁸ *But chose the tribe of Judah,*
The mount Zion which he loved.
⁶⁹ *And he built his sanctuary like the heights,*
Like the earth which he hath established for ever.
⁷⁰ *He chose David also his servant,*
And took him from the sheepfolds:
⁷¹ *From following the ewes that have their young he brought him,*
To be the shepherd of Jacob his people, and Israel his inheritance.
⁷² *So he was their shepherd according to the integrity of his heart,*
And guided them by the skilfulness of his hands.

We were given commandments
Handed down
From one generation to the next

We were called the children of God
That we might set our hearts aright

Our God divided the sea
And led us across deserts with a cloud
He brought streams out of the rocks

And still we sinned against him
And against ourselves

We did not believe in God
Or trust in him
We flattered him in his temples
And still we disobeyed the law
Forgetting we were but flesh
A wind that passes in front of us
Never to come this way again

In those days
It was we who did not remember him.

He destroyed our enemies in Egypt
Wrought his signs
Sent them pestilence
Wrecked their cattle
And their crops
And smote their firstborn

Or so the story goes

After waves of disobedience
And punishment
He chose us
We were the messengers of the one true God
We offered the world its deliverance
its laws
its moral code

And now we are punished
Forgotten
Disrespected
Waiting once again
For God to remember us
And through us

To remember the world

Psalm Seventy-nine

1 O God, the heathen are come into thine inheritance;
Thy holy temple have they defiled;
They have laid Jerusalem in heaps.
² The dead bodies of thy servants have they given to be food
Unto the birds of the heavens,
The flesh of thy saints unto the beasts of the earth.
³ Their blood have they shed like water round about Jerusalem;
And there was none to bury them.
⁴ We are become a reproach to our neighbors,
A scoffing and derision to them that are round about us.
⁵ How long, O God? wilt thou be angry for ever?
Shall thy jealousy burn like fire?
⁶ Pour out thy wrath upon the nations that know thee not,
And upon the kingdoms that call not upon thy name.
⁷ For they have devoured Jacob,
And laid waste his habitation.
⁸ Remember not against us the iniquities of our forefathers:
Let thy tender mercies speedily meet us;
For we are brought very low.
⁹ Help us, O God of our salvation, for the glory of thy name;
And deliver us, and forgive our sins, for thy name's sake.
¹⁰ Wherefore should the nations say, Where is their God?
Let the avenging of the blood of thy servants which is shed
Be known among the nations in our sight.
¹¹ Let the sighing of the prisoner come before thee:
According to the greatness of thy power preserve thou those
That are appointed to death;
¹² And render unto our neighbors sevenfold into their bosom
Their reproach, wherewith they have reproached thee, O Lord.
¹³ So we thy people and sheep of thy pasture
Will give thee thanks for ever:
We will show forth thy praise to all generations.

The heathen have come into their inheritance
They have defiled thy holy temples
And guffawed at you

There is no God
Proclaim the engineers
Scientists have known everything to know
For at least a hundred years
Survival of the fittest the presiding rule
Culling
Gleaning
Winnowing
Harvesting
A frankly superior race

In the meantime
Millions of Jews, Ukrainians, Poles, Tutsi, Han, Belgian Congolese
And moving right along
Left to right
And back again
Zulus, Sioux, Cherokee, Armenians
The New World Order
Stalin, Pol Pot, Mao
Shot, gassed, burned, mutilated, raped
To hell with it
Fill in the blanks

> *The blood of their people they have shed like water*

> *And there was none to bury them*

How long, O Lord
Till you show your face again?

Wherefore should the heathen say
Where is their God?
When you are gone
And hiding

And we are the disappeared

Psalm Eighty

1 Give ear, O Shepherd of Israel,
Thou that leadest Joseph like a flock;
Thou that sittest above the cherubim, shine forth.
² Before Ephraim and Benjamin and Manasseh, stir up thy might,
And come to save us.
³ Turn us again, O God;
And cause thy face to shine, and we shall be saved.
⁴ O God God of hosts,
How long wilt thou be angry against the prayer of thy people?
⁵ Thou hast fed them with the bread of tears,
And given them tears to drink in large measure.
⁶ Thou makest us a strife unto our neighbors;
And our enemies laugh among themselves.
⁷ Turn us again, O God of hosts;
And cause thy face to shine, and we shall be saved.
⁸ Thou broughtest a vine out of Egypt:
Thou didst drive out the nations, and plantedst it.
⁹ Thou preparedst room before it,
And it took deep root, and filled the land.
¹⁰ The mountains were covered with the shadow of it,
And the boughs thereof were like cedars of God.
¹¹ It sent out its branches unto the sea,
And its shoots unto the River.
¹² Why hast thou broken down its walls,
So that all they that pass by the way do pluck it?
¹³ The boar out of the wood doth ravage it,
And the wild beasts of the field feed on it.
¹⁴ Turn again, we beseech thee, O God of hosts:
Look down from heaven, and behold, and visit this vine,
¹⁵ And the stock which thy right hand planted,
And the branch that thou madest strong for thyself.
¹⁶ It is burned with fire, it is cut down:
They perish at the rebuke of thy countenance.

17 Let thy hand be upon the man of thy right hand,
Upon the son of man whom thou madest strong for thyself.
18 So shall we not go back from thee:
Quicken thou us, and we will call upon thy name.
19 Turn us again, O God God of hosts;
Cause thy face to shine, and we shall be saved.

Our enemies laugh at us
We hear

Clowns in fright wigs
And greasepaint
Rule the government
Our churches suffocate with pedophiles
And tears

Have we come this far
For what?

Our infrastructure falls apart
Bridges crumble
Kids go hungry
Roads collapse

What so proudly we hailed
In the home of the brave
Becomes an obstacle

Where are we now?
Where is the God of Israel
Where is The Lord of hosts?

When we were young
And prayed for strength
You guided us along the paths of righteousness
With liberty for all
We proclaimed
Under God
Indivisible

We had a dream
Didn't you?

Now we are given over to money
And the war machine
The military industrial leviathan
That sucks our brains
And eats our souls

O Lord God of hosts
Cause thy face to shine on us
And we shall be saved

Or is this another rain dance?
Another human sacrifice?

Psalm Eighty-one

1 Sing aloud unto God our strength:
Make a joyful noise unto the God of Jacob.
² Raise a song, and bring hither the timbrel,
The pleasant harp with the psaltery.
³ Blow the trumpet at the new moon,
At the full moon, on our feast-day.
⁴ For it is a statute for Israel,
An ordinance of the God of Jacob.
⁵ He appointed it in Joseph for a testimony,
When he went out over the land of Egypt,
Where I heard a language that I knew not.
⁶ I removed his shoulder from the burden:
His hands were freed from the basket.
⁷ Thou calledst in trouble, and I delivered thee;
I answered thee in the secret place of thunder;
I proved thee at the waters of Meribah. Selah
⁸ Hear, O my people, and I will testify unto thee:
O Israel, if thou wouldest hearken unto me!
⁹ There shall no strange god be in thee;
Neither shalt thou worship any foreign god.
¹⁰ I am God thy God,
Who brought thee up out of the land of Egypt:
Open thy mouth wide, and I will fill it.
¹¹ But my people hearkened not to my voice;
And Israel would none of me.
¹² So I let them go after the stubbornness of their heart,
That they might walk in their own counsels.
¹³ Oh that my people would hearken unto me,
That Israel would walk in my ways!
¹⁴ I would soon subdue their enemies,
And turn my hand against their adversaries.
¹⁵ The haters of God should submit themselves unto him:
But their time should endure for ever.

¹⁶ He would feed them also with the finest of the wheat;
And with honey out of the rock would I satisfy thee.

I would have destroyed your enemies
If you had come to me

Instead you kept your own counsels
And proclaimed there is no God
And went down in defeat

You forgot
You once called me in trouble
I delivered you from evil
And demolished your foe

I am the Lord thy God
Locked in silence
On the far side of Andromeda
Remembering what you have forgotten

Waiting for your return

Psalm Eighty-two

1 God standeth in the congregation of the mighty;
He judgeth among the gods.
² How long will ye judge unjustly,
And respect the persons of the wicked? Selah
³ Judge the poor and fatherless:
Do justice to the afflicted and destitute.
⁴ Rescue the poor and needy:
Deliver them out of the hand of the wicked.
⁵ They know not, neither do they understand;
They walk to and fro in darkness:
All the foundations of the earth are shaken.
⁶ I said, Ye are gods,
And all of you sons of the Most High.
⁷ Nevertheless ye shall die like men,
And fall like one of the princes.
⁸ Arise, O God, judge the earth;
For thou shalt inherit all the nations.

Deliver the poor and needy:
Rid them out of the hand of the wicked

Seems clear enough

Do justice to the afflicted

Clear

80 percent of prisoners today
Were raised without fathers

But undeniably
With plenty of God
And the rules of religion
Hallelujah

Praise the Lord
And keep it in your pants

They still walk on in darkness:
The foundations of the earth have veered off course

Who told us we were gods
Children of the Most High?

Why so much suffering?
Why so much disorder?
And litanies that make no sense
Except to priests and theologians?

Thoughts and prayers
We say
Every day
Thoughts and prayers

What about opening
The gates to the Bastille?

Psalm Eighty-three

1 O God, keep not thou silence:
Hold not thy peace, and be not still, O God.
² For, lo, thine enemies make a tumult;
And they that hate thee have lifted up the head.
³ They take crafty counsel against thy people,
And consult together against thy hidden ones.
⁴ They have said, Come, and let us cut them off from being a nation;
That the name of Israel may be no more in remembrance.
⁵ For they have consulted together with one consent;
Against thee do they make a covenant:
⁶ The tents of Edom and the Ishmaelites;
Moab, and the Hagarenes;
⁷ Gebal, and Ammon, and Amalek;
Philistia with the inhabitants of Tyre:
⁸ Assyria also is joined with them;
They have helped the children of Lot. Selah
⁹ Do thou unto them as unto Midian,
As to Sisera, as to Jabin, at the river Kishon;
¹⁰ Who perished at Endor,
Who became as dung for the earth.
¹¹ Make their nobles like Oreb and Zeeb;
Yea, all their princes like Zebah and Zalmunna;
¹² Who said, Let us take to ourselves in possession
The habitations of God.
¹³ O my God, make them like the whirling dust;
As stubble before the wind.
¹⁴ As the fire that burneth the forest,
And as the flame that setteth the mountains on fire,
¹⁵ So pursue them with thy tempest,
And terrify them with thy storm.
¹⁶ Fill their faces with confusion,
That they may seek thy name, O God.
¹⁷ Let them be put to shame and dismayed for ever;

Yea, let them be confounded and perish;
[18] *That they may know that thou alone, whose name is God,*
Art the Most High over all the earth.

Keep not thou silence, O God
Hold not thy peace
And be not still
Our enemies cause tumult
They plot against us
They buy up social media
They hack our nation from within

O God
Please be on our side
Burn down our enemies
Persecute them
Fill their brains with shame
And mutilation

Let them be confounded forever

If you really love us
If you really answer prayers

Or we will go to war
With waterboarding
Enhanced interrogation
Torture
And well disguised
Bio-chemical weapons

In the end
It's us or them

Isn't that the way?

Psalm Eighty-four

1 How amiable are thy tabernacles,
O God of hosts!
² My soul longeth, yea, even fainteth for the courts of God;
My heart and my flesh cry out unto the living God.
³ Yea, the sparrow hath found her a house,
And the swallow a nest for herself, where she may lay her young,
Even thine altars, O God of hosts,
My King, and my God.
⁴ Blessed are they that dwell in thy house:
They will be still praising thee. Selah
⁵ Blessed is the man whose strength is in thee;
In whose heart are the highways to Zion.
⁶ Passing through the valley of Weeping they make it a place of springs;
Yea, the early rain covereth it with blessings.
⁷ They go from strength to strength;
Every one of them appeareth before God in Zion.
⁸ O God God of hosts, hear my prayer;
Give ear, O God of Jacob. Selah
⁹ Behold, O God our shield,
And look upon the face of thine anointed.
¹⁰ For a day in thy courts is better than a thousand.
I had rather be a doorkeeper in the house of my God,
Than to dwell in the tents of wickedness.
¹¹ For God God is a sun and a shield:
God will give grace and glory;
No good thing will he withhold from them that walk uprightly.
¹² O God of hosts,
Blessed is the man that trusteth in thee.

Why do I spend my days
Longing for some unknown ghost
Of you
To permeate my heart?

Even sparrows rise at dawn
To sing with joy

Why do the faithful
Spend their days
In happiness
Or at least with equanimity?
They say they do

They are blessed
Who have found you
They go from strength to strength
Praising you
At least
They say they do

My flesh cries out for the living God
And the promises he made to us
My brain burns black with fire
I am trapped in the thicket of this marketplace
This labyrinth of loss and desire

O Lord of hosts
Blessed is the man that trusts in thee

Is that what you want to hear

Whoever you are?

Psalm Eighty-five

1 God, thou hast been favorable unto thy land;
Thou hast brought back the captivity of Jacob.
² Thou hast forgiven the iniquity of thy people;
Thou hast covered all their sin. Selah
³ Thou hast taken away all thy wrath;
Thou hast turned thyself from the fierceness of thine anger.
⁴ Turn us, O God of our salvation,
And cause thine indignation toward us to cease.
⁵ Wilt thou be angry with us for ever?
Wilt thou draw out thine anger to all generations?
⁶ Wilt thou not quicken us again,
That thy people may rejoice in thee?
⁷ Show us thy loving kindness, O God,
And grant us thy salvation.
⁸ I will hear what God God will speak;
For he will speak peace unto his people, and to his saints:
But let them not turn again to folly.
⁹ Surely his salvation is nigh them that fear him,
That glory may dwell in our land.
¹⁰ Mercy and truth are met together;
Righteousness and peace have kissed each other.
¹¹ Truth springeth out of the earth;
And righteousness hath looked down from heaven.
¹² Yea, God will give that which is good;
And our land shall yield its increase.
¹³ Righteousness shall go before him,
And shall make his footsteps a way to walk in.

We come from people
Who once believed in an angry God
An alpha male
High up in a darkened sky

Who would punish them
For any number
Of designated sins
The worst one
Worshipping other people's deities

Where are we now
With that ancestral Jove
That Yahweh
That G-d of intellectual voodoo
Inquisitional divinity

We still cry out for what we will never understand

Show us thy mercy, O Lord, and grant us thy salvation

We still believe
Truth shall spring out of the earth
And righteousness shall look down from above

Where does that leave us?

Have we abandoned our power to forgive?

Have we forsworn mercy
And forgotten our own hearts?

Psalm Eighty-six

1 Bow down thine ear, O God, and answer me;
For I am poor and needy.
² Preserve my soul; for I am godly:
O thou my God, save thy servant that trusteth in thee.
³ Be merciful unto me, O Lord;
For unto thee do I cry all the day long.
⁴ Rejoice the soul of thy servant;
For unto thee, O Lord, do I lift up my soul.
⁵ For thou, Lord, art good, and ready to forgive,
And abundant in loving kindness unto all them that call upon thee.
⁶ Give ear, O God, unto my prayer;
And hearken unto the voice of my supplications.
⁷ In the day of my trouble I will call upon thee;
For thou wilt answer me.
⁸ There is none like unto thee among the gods, O Lord;
Neither are there any works like unto thy works.
⁹ All nations whom thou hast made shall come
And worship before thee, O Lord;
And they shall glorify thy name.
¹⁰ For thou art great, and doest wondrous things:
Thou art God alone.
¹¹ Teach me thy way, O God; I will walk in thy truth:
Unite my heart to fear thy name.
¹² I will praise thee, O Lord my God, with my whole heart;
And I will glorify thy name for evermore.
¹³ For great is thy loving kindness toward me;
And thou hast delivered my soul from the lowest Sheol.
¹⁴ O God, the proud are risen up against me,
And a company of violent men have sought after my soul,
And have not set thee before them.
¹⁵ But thou, O Lord, art a God merciful and gracious,
Slow to anger, and abundant in loving kindness and truth.
¹⁶ Oh turn unto me, and have mercy upon me;

Give thy strength unto thy servant,
And save the son of thy handmaid.
[17] Show me a token for good,
That they who hate me may see it, and be put to shame,
Because thou, God, hast helped me, and comforted me.

I told Dr. Psychiatrist
I can figure this out myself

Besides
I said
You're too expensive
Too analytical
Much too serious
I said

In the meantime
I refuse to take my meds
I've read they make you suicidal
I'm already halfway there
On the fast road to institutional insanity
And ha ha
Hell

I stopped drinking
Days ago
Gave up gourmet food
Chocolate mousse
Patisserie
Amyl nitrate
Rocky Road
Hashish

That leaves God
To hear my prayers
And solve my problems
Presto change-o
Alakazam

By reputation
The idol in question
Is crammed with compassion
Gracious, longsuffering
Abundant in mercy and truth

Yes, I'm waiting for a reply

Jesus called him Father
Which might make sense
If you had one
That worked or
At least worked out

Otherwise, go with "Lord"
Which might apply

If you don't descend from generations
Of yeomen under the yoke
of medieval aristocracy

God

It's a problem

Psalm Eighty-seven

1 His foundation is in the holy mountains.
2 God loveth the gates of Zion
More than all the dwellings of Jacob.
3 Glorious things are spoken of thee, O city of God.
4 I will make mention of Rahab and Babylon
As among them that know me:
Behold, Philistia, and Tyre, with Ethiopia:
This one was born there.
5 Yea, of Zion it shall be said, This one and that one was born in her;
And the Most High himself will establish her.
6 God will count, when he writeth up the peoples,
This one was born there.
7 They that sing as well as they that dance shall say,
All my fountains are in thee.

The Indians claim there are two kinds of people.
One kind finds God in the mountains
The other at the sea

American Indians
Kemo Sabe
Not the red dot kind

FYI
The red dots have a lock on God
They find him everywhere
Everywhere and nowhere
Where there is nothing
There is God
Another conversation
Maybe another God

In the so-called wilderness
So-called God shows up in the mountains

With transfigurations
And tablets of stone
Take note
Writing down rules for the rest of us

I prefer to find him at the sea

The mother of life

And one day

hope to see him

once again

walking on the waves

Psalm Eighty-eight

1 O God, the God of my salvation,
I have cried day and night before thee.
² Let my prayer enter into thy presence;
Incline thine ear unto my cry.
³ For my soul is full of troubles,
And my life draweth nigh unto Sheol.
⁴ I am reckoned with them that go down into the pit;
I am as a man that hath no help,
⁵ Cast off among the dead,
Like the slain that lie in the grave,
Whom thou rememberest no more,
And they are cut off from thy hand.
⁶ Thou hast laid me in the lowest pit,
In dark places, in the deeps.
⁷ Thy wrath lieth hard upon me,
And thou hast afflicted me with all thy waves. Selah
⁸ Thou hast put mine acquaintance far from me;
Thou hast made me an abomination unto them:
I am shut up, and I cannot come forth.
⁹ Mine eye wasteth away by reason of affliction:
I have called daily upon thee, O God;
I have spread forth my hands unto thee.
¹⁰ Wilt thou show wonders to the dead?
Shall they that are deceased arise and praise thee? Selah
¹¹ Shall thy loving kindness be declared in the grave?
Or thy faithfulness in Destruction?
¹² Shall thy wonders be known in the dark?
And thy righteousness in the land of forgetfulness?
¹³ But unto thee, O God, have I cried;
And in the morning shall my prayer come before thee.
¹⁴ God, why castest thou off my soul?
Why hidest thou thy face from me?
¹⁵ I am afflicted and ready to die from my youth up:

While I suffer thy terrors I am distracted.
[16] Thy fierce wrath is gone over me;
Thy terrors have cut me off.
[17] They came round about me like water all the day long;
They compassed me about together.
[18] Lover and friend hast thou put far from me,
And mine acquaintance into darkness.

I cried for you

Now it's your turn to cry over me

I ain't got nobody
And other constraints
Care of clinical depression
Vaudeville
And a darkened world
Filled with egomaniacs
Narcissists
And way too many presidents

Why do I pray to a Fixer in the Sky?
Why do I expect him to answer me?
Why does he hide his face?
Why the terror?
Why the wrath?

Or is that just thunder and lightning
At the end of a perfect day?

Psalm Eighty-nine

1 I will sing of the loving kindness of God for ever:
With my mouth will I make known thy faithfulness to all generations.
² For I have said, Mercy shall be built up for ever;
Thy faithfulness wilt thou establish in the very heavens.
³ I have made a covenant with my chosen,
I have sworn unto David my servant:
⁴ Thy seed will I establish for ever,
And build up thy throne to all generations.
⁵ And the heavens shall praise thy wonders, O God;
Thy faithfulness also in the assembly of the holy ones.
⁶ For who in the skies can be compared unto God?
Who among the sons of the mighty is like unto God,
⁷ A God very terrible in the council of the holy ones,
And to be feared above all them that are round about him?
⁸ O God God of hosts,
Who is a mighty one, like unto thee, O God?
And thy faithfulness is round about thee.
⁹ Thou rulest the pride of the sea:
When the waves thereof arise, thou stillest them.
¹⁰ Thou hast broken Rahab in pieces, as one that is slain;
Thou hast scattered thine enemies with the arm of thy strength.
¹¹ The heavens are thine, the earth also is thine:
The world and the fulness thereof, thou hast founded them.
¹² The north and the south, thou hast created them:
Tabor and Hermon rejoice in thy name.
¹³ Thou hast a mighty arm;
Strong is thy hand, and high is thy right hand.
¹⁴ Righteousness and justice are the foundation of thy throne:
Loving kindness and truth go before thy face.
¹⁵ Blessed is the people that know the joyful sound:
They walk, O God, in the light of thy countenance.
¹⁶ In thy name do they rejoice all the day;
And in thy righteousness are they exalted.

[17] *For thou art the glory of their strength;*
And in thy favor our horn shall be exalted.
[18] *For our shield belongeth unto God;*
And our king to the Holy One of Israel.
[19] *Then thou spakest in vision to thy saints,*
And saidst, I have laid help upon one that is mighty;
I have exalted one chosen out of the people.
[20] *I have found David my servant;*
With my holy oil have I anointed him:
[21] *With whom my hand shall be established;*
Mine arm also shall strengthen him.
[22] *The enemy shall not exact from him,*
Nor the son of wickedness afflict him.
[23] *And I will beat down his adversaries before him,*
And smite them that hate him.
[24] *But my faithfulness and my loving kindness shall be with him;*
And in my name shall his horn be exalted.
[25] *I will set his hand also on the sea,*
And his right hand on the rivers.
[26] *He shall cry unto me, Thou art my Father,*
My God, and the rock of my salvation.
[27] *I also will make him my first-born,*
The highest of the kings of the earth.
[28] *My loving kindness will I keep for him for evermore;*
And my covenant shall stand fast with him.
[29] *His seed also will I make to endure for ever,*
And his throne as the days of heaven.
[30] *If his children forsake my law,*
And walk not in mine ordinances;
[31] *If they break my statutes,*
And keep not my commandments;
[32] *Then will I visit their transgression with the rod,*
And their iniquity with stripes.
[33] *But my loving kindness will I not utterly take from him,*
Nor suffer my faithfulness to fail.

³⁴ My covenant will I not break,
Nor alter the thing that is gone out of my lips.
³⁵ Once have I sworn by my holiness:
I will not lie unto David:
³⁶ His seed shall endure for ever,
And his throne as the sun before me.
³⁷ It shall be established for ever as the moon,
And as the faithful witness in the sky.
³⁸ But thou hast cast off and rejected,
Thou hast been wroth with thine anointed.
³⁹ Thou hast abhorred the covenant of thy servant:
Thou hast profaned his crown by casting it to the ground.
⁴⁰ Thou hast broken down all his hedges;
Thou hast brought his strongholds to ruin.
⁴¹ All that pass by the way rob him:
He is become a reproach to his neighbors.
⁴² Thou hast exalted the right hand of his adversaries;
Thou hast made all his enemies to rejoice.
⁴³ Yea, thou turnest back the edge of his sword,
And hast not made him to stand in the battle.
⁴⁴ Thou hast made his brightness to cease,
And cast his throne down to the ground.
⁴⁵ The days of his youth hast thou shortened:
Thou hast covered him with shame.
⁴⁶ How long, O God? wilt thou hide thyself for ever?
How long shall thy wrath burn like fire?
⁴⁷ Oh remember how short my time is:
For what vanity hast thou created all the children of men!
⁴⁸ What man is he that shall live and not see death,
That shall deliver his soul from the power of Sheol?
⁴⁹ Lord, where are thy former loving kindnesses,
Which thou swarest unto David in thy faithfulness?
⁵⁰ Remember, Lord, the reproach of thy servants;
How I do bear in my bosom the reproach of all the mighty peoples,
⁵¹ Wherewith thine enemies have reproached, O God,

Wherewith they have reproached the footsteps of thine anointed.
⁵² *Blessed be God for evermore.*
Amen, and Amen.

I sing of the Lord for ever and ever
And never shut up
An unrepentant fundamentalist
How's that?

I'm all for the Constitution
Word for word yessir
Not to mention
The Bible told me so

O Lord God of hosts
You rule the raging sea
You still the waves
And when you get around to it.
Which is to say
When it comes to war
You're on our side
Necessarily

You aim the missiles
You drop the bombs
With mercy
And with truth
Kaboom

A joyful noise unto the Lord
That's it

You raise up sons into the stratosphere
And daughters
After all, they're people too
Promising us prosperity
And almost immortality
Our seed shall last forever
Thanks to you

In the meantime
I'm still here

Blessed be the Lord for evermore
And evermore
Remember how short my time is, Lord

Don't forget

Amen

Psalm Ninety

1 Lord, thou hast been our dwelling-place
In all generations.
2 Before the mountains were brought forth,
Or ever thou hadst formed the earth and the world,
Even from everlasting to everlasting, thou art God.
3 Thou turnest man to destruction,
And sayest, Return, ye children of men.
4 For a thousand years in thy sight
Are but as yesterday when it is past,
And as a watch in the night.
5 Thou carriest them away as with a flood; they are as a sleep:
In the morning they are like grass which groweth up.
6 In the morning it flourisheth, and groweth up;
In the evening it is cut down, and withereth.
7 For we are consumed in thine anger,
And in thy wrath are we troubled.
8 Thou hast set our iniquities before thee,
Our secret sins in the light of thy countenance.
9 For all our days are passed away in thy wrath:
We bring our years to an end as a sigh.
10 The days of our years are threescore years and ten,
Or even by reason of strength fourscore years;
Yet is their pride but labor and sorrow;
For it is soon gone, and we fly away.
11 Who knoweth the power of thine anger,
And thy wrath according to the fear that is due unto thee?
12 So teach us to number our days,
That we may get us a heart of wisdom.
13 Return, O God; how long?
And let it repent thee concerning thy servants.
14 Oh satisfy us in the morning with thy loving kindness,
That we may rejoice and be glad all our days.
15 Make us glad according to the days wherein thou hast afflicted us,

And the years wherein we have seen evil.
¹⁶ Let thy work appear unto thy servants,
And thy glory upon their children.
¹⁷ And let the favor of the Lord our God be upon us;
And establish thou the work of our hands upon us;
Yea, the work of our hands establish thou it.

Outside of time
Outside of number
And measurement
And place

Outside of knowing
And reason

Beyond air
And light
And gravity

Is love

Do you believe?

It makes no difference

Love believes in you.

A thousand years are but as yesterday
A thousand sins are but as drops of rain

If you will but capitulate

Psalm Ninety-one

¹ *He that dwelleth in the secret place of the Most High*
Shall abide under the shadow of the Almighty.
² *I will say of God, He is my refuge and my fortress;*
My God, in whom I trust.
³ *For he will deliver thee from the snare of the fowler,*
And from the deadly pestilence.
⁴ *He will cover thee with his pinions,*
And under his wings shalt thou take refuge:
His truth is a shield and a buckler.
⁵ *Thou shalt not be afraid for the terror by night,*
Nor for the arrow that flieth by day;
⁶ *For the pestilence that walketh in darkness,*
Nor for the destruction that wasteth at noonday.
⁷ *A thousand shall fall at thy side,*
And ten thousand at thy right hand;
But it shall not come nigh thee.
⁸ *Only with thine eyes shalt thou behold,*
And see the reward of the wicked.
⁹ *For thou, O God, art my refuge!*
Thou hast made the Most High thy habitation;
¹⁰ *There shall no evil befall thee,*
Neither shall any plague come nigh thy tent.
¹¹ *For he will give his angels charge over thee,*
To keep thee in all thy ways.
¹² *They shall bear thee up in their hands,*
Lest thou dash thy foot against a stone.
¹³ *Thou shalt tread upon the lion and adder:*
The young lion and the serpent shalt thou trample under foot.
¹⁴ *Because he hath set his love upon me, therefore will I deliver him:*
I will set him on high, because he hath known my name.
¹⁵ *He shall call upon me, and I will answer him;*
I will be with him in trouble:
I will deliver him, and honor him.

¹⁶ With long life will I satisfy him,
And show him my salvation.

We live in the secret places of our heart
And call that God

We say we trust in him
What about trusting in ourselves?

Dare we call ourselves
Our refuge and our fortress?

Isn't it enough
To believe God knows our name?
Why do we expect him
To save us from the plague?

Still
Whether we believe it or not
And most of us say we don't

In the dark
At the end of our lives
We will call out his name
Asking him to deliver us from evil

And wait for him
To answer us

Psalm Ninety-two

1 It is a good thing to give thanks unto God,
And to sing praises unto thy name, O Most High;
² To show forth thy loving kindness in the morning,
And thy faithfulness every night,
³ With an instrument of ten strings, and with the psaltery;
With a solemn sound upon the harp.
⁴ For thou, God, hast made me glad through thy work:
I will triumph in the works of thy hands.
⁵ How great are thy works, O God!
Thy thoughts are very deep.
⁶ A brutish man knoweth not;
Neither doth a fool understand this:
⁷ When the wicked spring as the grass,
And when all the workers of iniquity do flourish;
It is that they shall be destroyed for ever.
⁸ But thou, O God, art on high for evermore.
⁹ For, lo, thine enemies, O God,
For, lo, thine enemies shall perish;
All the workers of iniquity shall be scattered.
¹⁰ But my horn hast thou exalted like the horn of the wild-ox:
I am anointed with fresh oil.
¹¹ Mine eye also hath seen my desire on mine enemies,
Mine ears have heard my desire of the evil-doers
That rise up against me.
¹² The righteous shall flourish like the palm-tree:
He shall grow like a cedar in Lebanon.
¹³ They are planted in the house of God;
They shall flourish in the courts of our God.
¹⁴ They shall still bring forth fruit in old age;
They shall be full of sap and green:
¹⁵ To show that God is upright;
He is my rock, and there is no unrighteousness in him.

Gratitude is the key
Singing comes second

Make your own Thanksgiving
For crab cakes
Shrimp 'n grits
Fried green tomatoes
Contact lenses
Licorice
Caesarians
Immunotherapy
Boykin spaniels
Licorice
Small claims court
The Wright Brothers
Mystics
Lake Wateree
Hollywood
Not necessary in that order
But definitely
One at a time
Or not

Like licorice

Order or chaos
Or linear reality
It all comes at once

The gorgeousness of the world
The splendor of the oceans
South Carolina in the spring

This time
Let me not fixate on iniquity

While the wicked wither like grass
The righteous shall flourish
Like a palm tree
Make that a Palmetto

Not to mention
Back yard gardens in the Battery
Here's to The Congaree
Willow oaks in Camden
The Swamp Rabbit Trail at Travelers Rest
Lake Marion
And the grace of Steeplechase

And here's to the rest of us

Glad to be alive

Psalm Ninety-three

1 God reigneth; he is clothed with majesty;
God is clothed with strength; he hath girded himself therewith:
The world also is established, that it cannot be moved.
² Thy throne is established of old:
Thou art from everlasting.
³ The floods have lifted up, O God,
The floods have lifted up their voice;
The floods lift up their waves.
⁴ Above the voices of many waters,
The mighty breakers of the sea,
God on high is mighty.
⁵ Thy testimonies are very sure:
Holiness becometh thy house,
O God, for evermore.

We want to believe in a world beyond ourselves
We want to live forever evermore
We want everything

We are made that way

Will our souls sing on the other side?
And dance?
Surely we will have music
A never-ending symphony
Of harmony, bel canto,
Hip hop, Broadway
And bluegrass

What about jazz?

Surely
We will love each other on the other side?

Who is this Sky God
This Spirit
This Presence
This Beloved?
What is this heaven in the clouds?

Who even wants a so-called other side
Without shrimp 'n grits
And passionate flesh?
As thanks for this most difficult ride

If we are to become insubstantial shades
Speaking for myself
If that's the case
Count me out

If that's the case
I intend to take a bow
And disappear

Goodbye

Psalm Ninety-four

1 O Lord God, thou God to whom vengeance belongeth,
Thou God to whom vengeance belongeth, shine forth.
² Lift up thyself, thou judge of the earth:
Render to the proud their desert.
³ God, how long shall the wicked,
How long shall the wicked triumph?
⁴ They prate, they speak arrogantly:
All the workers of iniquity boast themselves.
⁵ They break in pieces thy people, O God,
And afflict thy heritage.
⁶ They slay the widow and the sojourner,
And murder the fatherless.
⁷ And they say, God will not see,
Neither will the God of Jacob consider.
⁸ Consider, ye brutish among the people;
And ye fools, when will ye be wise?
⁹ He that planted the ear, shall he not hear?
He that formed the eye, shall he not see?
¹⁰ He that chastiseth the nations, shall not he correct,
Even he that teacheth man knowledge?
¹¹ God knoweth the thoughts of man,
That they are vanity.
¹² Blessed is the man whom thou chastenest, O God,
And teachest out of thy law;
¹³ That thou mayest give him rest from the days of adversity,
Until the pit be digged for the wicked.
¹⁴ For God will not cast off his people,
Neither will he forsake his inheritance.
¹⁵ For judgment shall return unto righteousness;
And all the upright in heart shall follow it.
¹⁶ Who will rise up for me against the evil-doers?
Who will stand up for me against the workers of iniquity?
¹⁷ Unless God had been my help,

My soul had soon dwelt in silence.
¹⁸ When I said, My foot slippeth;
Thy loving kindness, O God, held me up.
¹⁹ In the multitude of my thoughts within me
Thy comforts delight my soul.
²⁰ Shall the throne of wickedness have fellowship with thee,
Which frameth mischief by statute?
²¹ They gather themselves together against the soul of the righteous,
And condemn the innocent blood.
²² But God hath been my high tower,
And my God the rock of my refuge.
²³ And he hath brought upon them their own iniquity,
And will cut them off in their own wickedness;
God our God will cut them off.

How long can I feast on hate?

In the words of the Psalm
My enemies
Slay the widow and the stranger
They murder the fatherless

These days they send drones
To shoot up weddings
Of suspected terrorists

In the meantime
Bombing schools
And hospitals

Conjuring every excuse
To justify their appetite
For absolute control

I am fixated on wanting God
To exterminate the wicked

If he will not
If I am to be put upon
And the rest of us fall into death

I will dwell within mine soul
In silence

I will stand with myself

Once again

Alone

Psalm Ninety–five

1 Oh come, let us sing unto God;
Let us make a joyful noise to the rock of our salvation.
² Let us come before his presence with thanksgiving;
Let us make a joyful noise unto him with psalms.
³ For God is a great God,
And a great King above all gods.
⁴ In his hand are the deep places of the earth;
The heights of the mountains are his also.
⁵ The sea is his, and he made it;
And his hands formed the dry land.
⁶ Oh come, let us worship and bow down;
Let us kneel before God our Maker:
⁷ For he is our God,
And we are the people of his pasture, and the sheep of his hand.
To-day, oh that ye would hear his voice!
⁸ Harden not your heart, as at Meribah,
As in the day of Massah in the wilderness;
⁹ When your fathers tempted me,
Proved me, and saw my work.
¹⁰ Forty years long was I grieved with that generation,
And said, It is a people that do err in their heart,
And they have not known my ways:
¹¹ Wherefore I sware in my wrath,
That they should not enter into my rest.

O come, let us sing
Let us make a joyful noise.
Let us stand before life with gratitude
And wait for the voice within

> *For the Lord we have worshipped is a great God*
> *And a great King above all gods*

That's not the half of it

The Lord we have worshipped
Lo these millennia
Is a vengeful God
A tribal God
A God of us and them
Of black and white
Light and dark
Masters and slaves
A murderer

We deliberate about a God of love
Perhaps
Interpretation varies
Ruminations persist

Could there be another God beyond our God?
A God we do not know
Not yet
A presence we can only sense
A God encompassing all Gods
All intelligence
All questioning
A God our reason does not recognize
Only our inherent soul

Come let us listen for his voice
And if he has no voice
No sound
Except the wind
And the stirring of the earth

We will imagine him
Hoping for once
Our fantasy
Is real

Psalm Ninety–six

1 Oh sing unto God a new song:
Sing unto God, all the earth.
² Sing unto God, bless his name;
Show forth his salvation from day to day.
³ Declare his glory among the nations,
His marvellous works among all the peoples.
⁴ For great is God, and greatly to be praised:
He is to be feared above all gods.
⁵ For all the gods of the peoples are idols;
But God made the heavens.
⁶ Honor and majesty are before him:
Strength and beauty are in his sanctuary.
⁷ Ascribe unto God, ye kindreds of the peoples,
Ascribe unto God glory and strength.
⁸ Ascribe unto God the glory due unto his name:
Bring an offering, and come into his courts.
⁹ Oh worship God in holy array:
Tremble before him, all the earth.
¹⁰ Say among the nations, God reigneth:
The world also is established that it cannot be moved:
He will judge the peoples with equity.
¹¹ Let the heavens be glad, and let the earth rejoice;
Let the sea roar, and the fulness thereof;
¹² Let the field exult, and all that is therein;
Then shall all the trees of the wood sing for joy
¹³ Before God; for he cometh,
For he cometh to judge the earth:
He will judge the world with righteousness,
And the peoples with his truth.

Our God clutches
Counter-electronics high-power advanced microwaves
And nuclear bombs

He employs
Stealthy joint air-to-surface standoff missile-extended range delivery
Vehicles
With murderous intent

This God is to be feared

You think?

Majesty lies before him.
He made the heavens sing
The oceans roar
The fields rejoice
He will vanquish his enemies
And obliterate his foes

Whatever you do
Bring offerings
Especially yourselves
Your bone and blood and breath

What is your life
And your childrens' lives
Compared to his?

All praise to the destroyer god
Kali
Yahweh
Thor

Whatever the name
They're all the same

The Absolute Destroyer rules

Psalm Ninety-seven

1 God reigneth; let the earth rejoice;
Let the multitude of isles be glad.
² Clouds and darkness are round about him:
Righteousness and justice are the foundation of his throne.
³ A fire goeth before him,
And burneth up his adversaries round about.
⁴ His lightnings lightened the world:
The earth saw, and trembled.
⁵ The mountains melted like wax at the presence of God,
At the presence of the Lord of the whole earth.
⁶ The heavens declare his righteousness,
And all the peoples have seen his glory.
⁷ Let all them be put to shame that serve graven images,
That boast themselves of idols:
Worship him, all ye gods.
⁸ Zion heard and was glad,
And the daughters of Judah rejoiced,
Because of thy judgments, O God.
⁹ For thou, God, art most high above all the earth:
Thou art exalted far above all gods.
¹⁰ O ye that love God, hate evil:
He preserveth the souls of his saints;
He delivereth them out of the hand of the wicked.
¹¹ Light is sown for the righteous,
And gladness for the upright in heart.
¹² Be glad in God, ye righteous;
And give thanks to his holy memorial name.

Aside from gunmen arriving at our door
Automatic arsenals in hand
Burning down our domiciles
Breaking skulls
Slaughtering children

Do we need governments to tell us
Who our opponents are
Much less the religious establishment?

The Lord burneth up his enemies
According to scriptural truth
Revealed forever in a burning bush
A cynical judgment without a doubt
What recourse do we have?
Which way out?

About the world trembling before the Lord
What kind of god is that?
How far have we progressed from Zeus and Baal?

Our lord is righteous
Is that it?
Our God is better than theirs
Holier
Angrier

Yes?

Most importantly
Our God is ours

Oh good

Psalm Ninety-eight

1 Oh sing unto God a new song;
For he hath done marvellous things:
His right hand, and his holy arm, hath wrought salvation for him.
² God hath made known his salvation:
His righteousness hath he openly showed in the sight of the nations.
³ He hath remembered his loving kindness
And his faithfulness toward the house of Israel:
All the ends of the earth have seen the salvation of our God.
⁴ Make a joyful noise unto God, all the earth:
Break forth and sing for joy, yea, sing praises.
⁵ Sing praises unto God with the harp;
With the harp and the voice of melody.
⁶ With trumpets and sound of cornet
Make a joyful noise before the King, God.
⁷ Let the sea roar, and the fulness thereof;
The world, and they that dwell therein;
⁸ Let the floods clap their hands;
Let the hills sing for joy together
⁹ Before God; for he cometh to judge the earth:
He will judge the world with righteousness,
And the peoples with equity.

Why is civilization predicated
On an anthropomorphic deity?

Take a breath

To disavow this predictable conceit
About a Sky God
Who's promised to return one day
To bestow mercy on our chosen selves
And trample on our enemies
One risks being called
A village atheist

Another breath

Sing out to the Lord they say
They the institutional
One True Faith
Looking for tithes
Advertising miracles

And no doubt obedience

I sing out to myself
Not to any deity

I sing to keep my courage up
Accompanied
By trumpets and cornets
And the roaring of the sea

All to distract me

From the awful silence that is God.

Psalm Ninety-nine

1 God reigneth; let the peoples tremble:
He sitteth above the cherubim; let the earth be moved.
² God is great in Zion;
And he is high above all the peoples.
³ Let them praise thy great and terrible name:
Holy is he.

⁴ The king's strength also loveth justice;
Thou dost establish equity;
Thou executest justice and righteousness in Jacob.
⁵ Exalt ye God our God,
And worship at his footstool:
Holy is he.

⁶ Moses and Aaron among his priests,
And Samuel among them that call upon his name;
They called upon God, and he answered them.
⁷ He spake unto them in the pillar of cloud:
They kept his testimonies,
And the statute that he gave them.
⁸ Thou answeredst them, O God our God:
Thou wast a God that forgavest them,
Though thou tookest vengeance of their doings.
⁹ Exalt ye God our God,
And worship at his holy hill;
For God our God is holy.

I have heard your name is great and terrible

A worst-case scenario

Worse than the mercy of the human race
Forever up for sale

And the force of the king
Obsessively at war

We exalt the Lord our God
That would be you
For what reason
We do not yet understand

You, at least in theory
Are complete unto yourself

Will you protect us
Against ourselves?

Will you teach us
A better way
Than our usual pursuits?

They say you sitteth between the cherubims
Fat little angels with flightless wings
Some with sweetheart faces
Others looking like lions and bulls

Theologians
Who could be building bridges
And growing food
Or at least playing blackjack
Spend lifetimes
Discussing God
The invisible
The silent

And the unknown

Psalm One hundred

1 Make a joyful noise unto God, all ye lands.
² Serve God with gladness:
Come before his presence with singing.
³ Know ye that God, he is God:
It is he that hath made us, and we are his;
We are his people, and the sheep of his pasture.
⁴ Enter into his gates with thanksgiving,
And into his courts with praise:
Give thanks unto him, and bless his name.
⁵ For God is good; his loving kindness endureth for ever,
And his faithfulness unto all generations.

We did not make ourselves
Theologians say
They
Or ministers who pick up snakes
Or even evolutionists
Okay

We did not invent
Archaic terminology
That speaks of lords and gods
And the gates
To everlasting bliss

Beyond fantasy and make-believe
What does our imagination know?
How real is possibility?

What is the deeper meaning of a kiss?

Psalm One hundred one

1 I will sing of loving kindness and justice:
Unto thee, O God, will I sing praises.
² I will behave myself wisely in a perfect way:
Oh when wilt thou come unto me?
I will walk within my house with a perfect heart.
³ I will set no base thing before mine eyes:
I hate the work of them that turn aside;
It shall not cleave unto me.
⁴ A perverse heart evil thing.
⁵ Whoso privily shall depart from me:
I will know no slandereth his neighbor, him will I destroy:
Him that hath a high look and a proud heart will I not suffer.
⁶ Mine eyes shall be upon the faithful of the land,
That they may dwell with me:
He that walketh in a perfect way, he shall minister unto me.
⁷ He that worketh deceit shall not dwell within my house:
He that speaketh falsehood shall not be established before mine eyes.
⁸ Morning by morning will I destroy all the wicked of the land;
To cut off all the workers of iniquity from the city of God.

Some people have a jolly time
Avoiding alcohol
Prescription drugs
And cigarettes
Not to mention calories
And fun

My problem is avoiding
Narcissists

Their life is all about them
Understood
In their enlightened view
My life is all about them too

History and psychology
Biology
Astrology
Nuclear physics
All about them

They remember
Every slight
Real or imagined
And sometimes
But not often
Compliments
Why not?

I tell them they're magnificent
Glorious
Superb
Emphasizing every syllable

I reassure them
Encourage them
Hold their hand
And by degrees
I cease to be

I'm talking about me and God
At least the deity
Who's been described to me

They say I'm losing my memory

I say I'm losing my mind

Good thing

Psalm One hundred two

1 Hear my prayer, O God,
And let my cry come unto thee.
² Hide not thy face from me in the day of my distress:
Incline thine ear unto me;
In the day when I call answer me speedily.
³ For my days consume away like smoke,
And my bones are burned as a firebrand.
⁴ My heart is smitten like grass, and withered;
For I forget to eat my bread.
⁵ By reason of the voice of my groaning
My bones cleave to my flesh.
⁶ I am like a pelican of the wilderness;
I am become as an owl of the waste places.
⁷ I watch, and am become like a sparrow
That is alone upon the house-top.
⁸ Mine enemies reproach me all the day;
They that are mad against me do curse by me.
⁹ For I have eaten ashes like bread,
And mingled my drink with weeping,
¹⁰ Because of thine indignation and thy wrath:
For thou hast taken me up, and cast me away.
¹¹ My days are like a shadow that declineth;
And I am withered like grass.
¹² But thou, O God, wilt abide for ever;
And thy memorial name unto all generations.
¹³ Thou wilt arise, and have mercy upon Zion;
For it is time to have pity upon her,
Yea, the set time is come.
¹⁴ For thy servants take pleasure in her stones,
And have pity upon her dust.
¹⁵ So the nations shall fear the name of God,
And all the kings of the earth thy glory.
¹⁶ For God hath built up Zion;

He hath appeared in his glory.
[17] He hath regarded the prayer of the destitute,
And hath not despised their prayer.
[18] This shall be written for the generation to come;
And a people which shall be created shall praise God.
[19] For he hath looked down from the height of his sanctuary;
From heaven did God behold the earth;
[20] To hear the sighing of the prisoner;
To loose those that are appointed to death;
[21] That men may declare the name of God in Zion,
And his praise in Jerusalem;
[22] When the peoples are gathered together,
And the kingdoms, to serve God.
[23] He weakened my strength in the way;
He shortened my days.
[24] I said, O my God, take me not away in the midst of my days:
Thy years are throughout all generations.
[25] Of old didst thou lay the foundation of the earth;
And the heavens are the work of thy hands.
[26] They shall perish, but thou shalt endure;
Yea, all of them shall wax old like a garment;
As a vesture shalt thou change them, and they shall be changed:
[27] But thou art the same,
And thy years shall have no end.
[28] The children of thy servants shall continue,
And their seed shall be established before thee.

My days are spent like smoke
My heart withered like dead grass

I sit alone on the rooftop weeping
Heading to the end of my days

It is written
Thou hast laid the foundation of the earth
The heavens are the work of thy hands

It is said you shall endure forever
Remembered unto all generations
Could this possibly be true?

They say you hear the groaning of the prisoners
You regard the prayers of the destitute
And those appointed unto death

And then?

O my God
Take me not away in the midst of my days
Thou art the same
Thy years shall have no end

Ah yes

Are these deliberations
Merely
The imagination of the earth
The dreams of prisoners
The insistence of the ridiculous?

Surely, hope marches forward
With authority
Surely, dreams are real

Surely, we can own desire

Psalm One hundred three

1 Bless God, O my soul;
And all that is within me, bless his holy name.
² Bless God, O my soul,
And forget not all his benefits:
³ Who forgiveth all thine iniquities;
Who healeth all thy diseases;
⁴ Who redeemeth thy life from destruction;
Who crowneth thee with loving kindness and tender mercies;
⁵ Who satisfieth thy desire with good things,
So that thy youth is renewed like the eagle.
⁶ God executeth righteous acts,
And judgments for all that are oppressed.
⁷ He made known his ways unto Moses,
His doings unto the children of Israel.
⁸ God is merciful and gracious,
Slow to anger, and abundant in loving kindness.
⁹ He will not always chide;
Neither will he keep his anger for ever.
¹⁰ He hath not dealt with us after our sins,
Nor rewarded us after our iniquities.
¹¹ For as the heavens are high above the earth,
So great is his loving kindness toward them that fear him.
¹² As far as the east is from the west,
So far hath he removed our transgressions from us.
¹³ Like as a father pitieth his children,
So God pitieth them that fear him.
¹⁴ For he knoweth our frame;
He remembereth that we are dust.
¹⁵ As for man, his days are as grass;
As a flower of the field, so he flourisheth.
¹⁶ For the wind passeth over it, and it is gone;
And the place thereof shall know it no more.
¹⁷ But the loving kindness of God is from everlasting

To everlasting upon them that fear him,
And his righteousness unto children's children;
[18] *To such as keep his covenant,*
And to those that remember his precepts to do them.
[19] *God hath established his throne in the heavens;*
And his kingdom ruleth over all.
[20] *Bless God, ye his angels,*
That are mighty in strength, that fulfil his word,
Hearkening unto the voice of his word.
[21] *Bless God, all ye his hosts,*
Ye ministers of his, that do his pleasure.
[22] *Bless God, all ye his works,*
In all places of his dominion:
Bless God, O my soul.

There is a spirit
Alive in the land
That forgives iniquities
And heals disease.

There is a mood
That comes with kindness
And mercy
Slow to anger
Gracious in all things

There is a mind abroad
That remembers we are dust
Our days like grass
When the wind passes over us
And we are gone

There is a remembering
Angels will come again
And bless the worst of us

And a holy mother
Will hold us in her arms
And pray with us
At the hour of our death

Amen

Psalm One hundred four

1 Bless God, O my soul.
O God my God, thou art very great;
Thou art clothed with honor and majesty:
² Who coverest thyself with light as with a garment;
Who stretchest out the heavens like a curtain;
³ Who layeth the beams of his chambers in the waters;
Who maketh the clouds his chariot;
Who walketh upon the wings of the wind;
⁴ Who maketh winds his messengers;
Flames of fire his ministers;
⁵ Who laid the foundations of the earth,
That it should not be moved for ever.
⁶ Thou coveredst it with the deep as with a vesture;
The waters stood above the mountains.
⁷ At thy rebuke they fled;
At the voice of thy thunder they hasted away
⁸ The mountains rose, the valleys sank down)
Unto the place which thou hadst founded for them.
⁹ Thou hast set a bound that they may not pass over;
That they turn not again to cover the earth.
¹⁰ He sendeth forth springs into the valleys;
They run among the mountains;
¹¹ They give drink to every beast of the field;
The wild asses quench their thirst.
¹² By them the birds of the heavens have their habitation;
They sing among the branches.
¹³ He watereth the mountains from his chambers:
The earth is filled with the fruit of thy works.
¹⁴ He causeth the grass to grow for the cattle,
And herb for the service of man;
That he may bring forth food out of the earth,
¹⁵ And wine that maketh glad the heart of man,
And oil to make his face to shine,

And bread that strengtheneth man's heart.
¹⁶ The trees of God are filled with moisture,
The cedars of Lebanon, which he hath planted;
¹⁷ Where the birds make their nests:
As for the stork, the fir-trees are her house.
¹⁸ The high mountains are for the wild goats;
The rocks are a refuge for the conies.
¹⁹ He appointed the moon for seasons:
The sun knoweth his going down.
²⁰ Thou makest darkness, and it is night,
Wherein all the beasts of the forest creep forth.
²¹ The young lions roar after their prey,
And seek their food from God.
²² The sun ariseth, they get them away,
And lay them down in their dens.
²³ Man goeth forth unto his work
And to his labor until the evening.
²⁴ O God, how manifold are thy works!
In wisdom hast thou made them all:
The earth is full of thy riches.
²⁵ Yonder is the sea, great and wide,
Wherein are things creeping innumerable,
Both small and great beasts.
²⁶ There go the ships;
There is leviathan, whom thou hast formed to play therein.
²⁷ These wait all for thee,
That thou mayest give them their food in due season.
²⁸ Thou givest unto them, they gather;
Thou openest thy hand, they are satisfied with good.
²⁹ Thou hidest thy face, they are troubled;
Thou takest away their breath, they die,
And return to their dust.
³⁰ Thou sendest forth thy Spirit, they are created;
And thou renewest the face of the ground.
³¹ Let the glory of God endure for ever;
Let God rejoice in his works:

³² *Who looketh on the earth, and it trembleth;*
He toucheth the mountains, and they smoke.
³³ *I will sing unto God as long as I live:*
I will sing praise to my God while I have any being.
³⁴ *Let my meditation be sweet unto him:*
I will rejoice in God.
³⁵ *Let sinners be consumed out of the earth.*
And let the wicked be no more.
Bless God, O my soul.
Praise ye God.

The ancients
From whom we come
Believed the earth
Was the body of the god
Or better yet
The goddess
Yes

She is Gaia
Wrapped in light
And darkness too
Shimmering
In the wind and rain

The beasts of the fields
The birds in the forests
Sing in exultation

We drink in the beauty
You have given us
You water the hills
And cause the grass to grow
That we may bring forth food
And wine
And bread that strengthens us

Gaia
Now is our hour of need
Breathe forth your spirit
And renew the face of Earth

As long as we live
We will sing your praise and be glad

We look on the earth and it trembles
We touch the hills and they smoke

We sing your name

Amen

Psalm One hundred five

1 Oh give thanks unto God, call upon his name;
Make known among the peoples his doings.
² Sing unto him, sing praises unto him;
Talk ye of all his marvellous works.
³ Glory ye in his holy name:
Let the heart of them rejoice that seek God.
⁴ Seek ye God and his strength;
Seek his face evermore.
⁵ Remember his marvellous works that he hath done,
His wonders, and the judgments of his mouth,
⁶ O ye seed of Abraham his servant,
Ye children of Jacob, his chosen ones.
⁷ He is God our God:
His judgments are in all the earth.
⁸ He hath remembered his covenant for ever,
The word which he commanded to a thousand generations,
⁹ The covenant which he made with Abraham,
And his oath unto Isaac,
¹⁰ And confirmed the same unto Jacob for a statute,
To Israel for an everlasting covenant,
¹¹ Saying, Unto thee will I give the land of Canaan,
The lot of your inheritance;
¹² When they were but a few men in number,
Yea, very few, and sojourners in it.
¹³ And they went about from nation to nation,
From one kingdom to another people.
¹⁴ He suffered no man to do them wrong;
Yea, he reproved kings for their sakes,
¹⁵ Saying, Touch not mine anointed ones,
And do my prophets no harm.
¹⁶ And he called for a famine upon the land;
He brake the whole staff of bread.
¹⁷ He sent a man before them;

Joseph was sold for a servant:
¹⁸ His feet they hurt with fetters:
He was laid in chains of iron,
¹⁹ Until the time that his word came to pass,
The word of God tried him.
²⁰ The king sent and loosed him;
Even the ruler of peoples, and let him go free.
²¹ He made him lord of his house,
And ruler of all his substance;
²² To bind his princes at his pleasure,
And teach his elders wisdom.
²³ Israel also came into Egypt;
And Jacob sojourned in the land of Ham.
²⁴ And he increased his people greatly,
And made them stronger than their adversaries.
²⁵ He turned their heart to hate his people,
To deal subtly with his servants.
²⁶ He sent Moses his servant,
And Aaron whom he had chosen.
²⁷ They set among them his signs,
And wonders in the land of Ham.
²⁸ He sent darkness, and made it dark;
And they rebelled not against his words.
²⁹ He turned their waters into blood,
And slew their fish.
³⁰ Their land swarmed with frogs
In the chambers of their kings.
³¹ He spake, and there came swarms of flies,
And lice in all their borders.
³² He gave them hail for rain,
And flaming fire in their land.
³³ He smote their vines also and their fig-trees,
And brake the trees of their borders.
³⁴ He spake, and the locust came,
And the grasshopper, and that without number,
³⁵ And did eat up every herb in their land,

And did eat up the fruit of their ground.
[36] *He smote also all the first-born in their land,*
The chief of all their strength.
[37] *And he brought them forth with silver and gold;*
And there was not one feeble person among his tribes.
[38] *Egypt was glad when they departed;*
For the fear of them had fallen upon them.
[39] *He spread a cloud for a covering,*
And fire to give light in the night.
[40] *They asked, and he brought quails,*
And satisfied them with the bread of heaven.
[41] *He opened the rock, and waters gushed out;*
They ran in the dry places like a river.
[42] *For he remembered his holy word,*
And Abraham his servant.
[43] *And he brought forth his people with joy,*
And his chosen with singing.
[44] *And he gave them the lands of the nations;*
And they took the labor of the peoples in possession:
[45] *That they might keep his statutes,*
And observe his laws.
Praise ye God.

Give thanks to the Jews
Celebrate the people of the book
Do not bow low to an idol in the sky

The children of Israel
Have made us understand
We need not be worshipping the sun
The moon
The gods in the forest
And the sea

However obvious in the telling
Yahweh came to earth

A warrior deity
Drenched in the blood of enemies

After Abraham
Listen up
Theology, so called
Continued to evolve

His chosen people—
They chose themselves
Should not everyone choose themselves?
Have through the succeeding centuries
Brought justice to earth
Compassion to strangers
Light to the shadows
And beauty to the night

Jews are the givers
That is their covenant
Between I Am Who Am
And the world of flesh
And mud
And the human heart

They have given us prophets
Scholars
And seers
To lead us from the lands
Of darkness
And blood
Into a place of questioning

The life of the mind

L'Chaim!

Psalm One hundred six

1 Praise ye God.
Oh give thanks unto God; for he is good;
For his loving kindness endureth for ever.
² Who can utter the mighty acts of God,
Or show forth all his praise?
³ Blessed are they that keep justice,
And he that doeth righteousness at all times.
⁴ Remember me, O God, with the favor
That thou bearest unto thy people;
Oh visit me with thy salvation,
⁵ That I may see the prosperity of thy chosen,
That I may rejoice in the gladness of thy nation,
That I may glory with thine inheritance.
⁶ We have sinned with our fathers,
We have committed iniquity, we have done wickedly.
⁷ Our fathers understood not thy wonders in Egypt;
They remembered not the multitude of thy loving kindnesses,
But were rebellious at the sea, even at the Red Sea.
⁸ Nevertheless he saved them for his name's sake,
That he might make his mighty power to be known.
⁹ He rebuked the Red Sea also, and it was dried up:
So he led them through the depths, as through a wilderness.
¹⁰ And he saved them from the hand of him that hated them,
And redeemed them from the hand of the enemy.
¹¹ And the waters covered their adversaries;
There was not one of them left.
¹² Then believed they his words;
They sang his praise.
¹³ They soon forgat his works;
They waited not for his counsel,
¹⁴ But lusted exceedingly in the wilderness,
And tempted God in the desert.
¹⁵ And he gave them their request,

But sent leanness into their soul.
[16] *They envied Moses also in the camp,*
And Aaron the saint of God.
[17] *The earth opened and swallowed up Dathan,*
And covered the company of Abiram.
[18] *And a fire was kindled in their company;*
The flame burned up the wicked.
[19] *They made a calf in Horeb,*
And worshipped a molten image.
[20] *Thus they changed their glory*
For the likeness of an ox that eateth grass.
[21] *They forgat God their Saviour,*
Who had done great things in Egypt,
[22] *Wondrous works in the land of Ham,*
And terrible things by the Red Sea.
[23] *Therefore he said that he would destroy them,*
Had not Moses his chosen stood before him in the breach,
To turn away his wrath, lest he should destroy them.
[24] *Yea, they despised the pleasant land,*
They believed not his word,
[25] *But murmured in their tents,*
And hearkened not unto the voice of God.
[26] *Therefore he sware unto them,*
That he would overthrow them in the wilderness,
[27] *And that he would overthrow their seed among the nations,*
And scatter them in the lands.
[28] *They joined themselves also unto Baal-peor,*
And ate the sacrifices of the dead.
[29] *Thus they provoked him to anger with their doings;*
And the plague brake in upon them.
[30] *Then stood up Phinehas, and executed judgment;*
And so the plague was stayed.
[31] *And that was reckoned unto him for righteousness,*
Unto all generations for evermore.
[32] *They angered him also at the waters of Meribah,*
So that it went ill with Moses for their sakes;

⁣³³ *Because they were rebellious against his spirit,*
And he spake unadvisedly with his lips.
³⁴ *They did not destroy the peoples,*
As God commanded them,
³⁵ *But mingled themselves with the nations,*
And learned their works,
³⁶ *And served their idols,*
Which became a snare unto them.
³⁷ *Yea, they sacrificed their sons and their daughters unto demons,*
³⁸ *And shed innocent blood,*
Even the blood of their sons and of their daughters,
Whom they sacrificed unto the idols of Canaan;
And the land was polluted with blood.
³⁹ *Thus were they defiled with their works,*
And played the harlot in their doings.
⁴⁰ *Therefore was the wrath of God kindled against his people,*
And he abhorred his inheritance.
⁴¹ *And he gave them into the hand of the nations;*
And they that hated them ruled over them.
⁴² *Their enemies also oppressed them,*
And they were brought into subjection under their hand.
⁴³ *Many times did he deliver them;*
But they were rebellious in their counsel,
And were brought low in their iniquity.
⁴⁴ *Nevertheless he regarded their distress,*
When he heard their cry:
⁴⁵ *And he remembered for them his covenant,*
And repented according to the multitude of his loving kindnesses.
⁴⁶ *He made them also to be pitied*
Of all those that carried them captive.
⁴⁷ *Save us, O God our God,*
And gather us from among the nations,
To give thanks unto thy holy name,
And to triumph in thy praise.
⁴⁸ *Blessed be God, the God of Israel,*

From everlasting even to everlasting.
And let all the people say, Amen
Praise ye God.

We labored in the mines
And beseeched you
Until our lungs turned black

And where were you?

We toiled in the fields
Through drought and pestilence
The dust rose up
And drove us to despair
All the while we praised your holy name

And you?

Crops failed one year into the next
Children born dead
And still we prayed
Expecting happier times
And better endings
We suffered
Disease and desperation
Still we gave you praise
And thanks
With no response

Except for the moon and the stars
And the beauty of the land
And the love we bore one another

And that was nearly enough

Wasn't it?

We forgive you for making us mortal
We forgive you for hiding your face
We have forgiven your silence
Your resistance to reason
And common decency

We are surrounded
By those who say there is no God
Who say
There is no plan
No universal mind

Remember us
Remember your covenant
Do not abandon us
Blessed be the Lord God of Israel from everlasting to everlasting
Praise ye the Lord
Let all the people say Amen

Psalm One hundred seven

1 Oh give thanks unto God; for he is good;
For his loving kindness endureth for ever.
² Let the redeemed of God say so,
Whom he hath redeemed from the hand of the adversary,
³ And gathered out of the lands,
From the east and from the west,
From the north and from the south.
⁴ They wandered in the wilderness in a desert way;
They found no city of habitation.
⁵ Hungry and thirsty,
Their soul fainted in them.
⁶ Then they cried unto God in their trouble,
And he delivered them out of their distresses,
⁷ He led them also by a straight way,
That they might go to a city of habitation.
⁸ Oh that men would praise God for his loving kindness,
And for his wonderful works to the children of men!
⁹ For he satisfieth the longing soul,
And the hungry soul he filleth with good.
¹⁰ Such as sat in darkness and in the shadow of death,
Being bound in affliction and iron,
¹¹ Because they rebelled against the words of God,
And contemned the counsel of the Most High:
¹² Therefore he brought down their heart with labor;
They fell down, and there was none to help.
¹³ Then they cried unto God in their trouble,
And he saved them out of their distresses.
¹⁴ He brought them out of darkness and the shadow of death,
And brake their bonds in sunder.
¹⁵ Oh that men would praise God for his loving kindness,
And for his wonderful works to the children of men!
¹⁶ For he hath broken the gates of brass,
And cut the bars of iron in sunder.

¹⁷ *Fools because of their transgression,*
And because of their iniquities, are afflicted.
¹⁸ *Their soul abhorreth all manner of food;*
And they draw near unto the gates of death.
¹⁹ *Then they cry unto God in their trouble,*
And he saveth them out of their distresses.
²⁰ *He sendeth his word, and healeth them,*
And delivereth them from their destructions.
²¹ *Oh that men would praise God for his loving kindness,*
And for his wonderful works to the children of men!
²² *And let them offer the sacrifices of thanksgiving,*
And declare his works with singing.
²³ *They that go down to the sea in ships,*
That do business in great waters;
²⁴ *These see the works of God,*
And his wonders in the deep.
²⁵ *For he commandeth, and raiseth the stormy wind,*
Which lifteth up the waves thereof.
²⁶ *They mount up to the heavens, they go down again to the depths:*
Their soul melteth away because of trouble.
²⁷ *They reel to and fro, and stagger like a drunken man,*
And are at their wits' end.
²⁸ *Then they cry unto God in their trouble,*
And he bringeth them out of their distresses.
²⁹ *He maketh the storm a calm,*
So that the waves thereof are still.
³⁰ *Then are they glad because they are quiet;*
So he bringeth them unto their desired haven.
³¹ *Oh that men would praise God for his loving kindness,*
And for his wonderful works to the children of men!
³² *Let them exalt him also in the assembly of the people,*
And praise him in the seat of the elders.
³³ *He turneth rivers into a wilderness,*
And watersprings into a thirsty ground;
³⁴ *A fruitful land into a salt desert,*

For the wickedness of them that dwell therein.
³⁵ He turneth a wilderness into a pool of water,
And a dry land into watersprings.
³⁶ And there he maketh the hungry to dwell,
That they may prepare a city of habitation,
³⁷ And sow fields, and plant vineyards,
And get them fruits of increase.
³⁸ He blesseth them also, so that they are multiplied greatly;
And he suffereth not their cattle to decrease.
³⁹ Again, they are diminished and bowed down
Through oppression, trouble, and sorrow.
⁴⁰ He poureth contempt upon princes,
And causeth them to wander in the waste, where there is no way.
⁴¹ Yet setteth he the needy on high from affliction,
And maketh him families like a flock.
⁴² The upright shall see it, and be glad;
And all iniquity shall stop her mouth.
⁴³ Whoso is wise will give heed to these things;
And they will consider the loving kindnesses of God.

We of this human tribe
Have wandered in the wilderness
And found no city to dwell in

Hungry and thirsty
Our souls have wasted away
Until we cried upon the Lord

According to the ancient memories
At the moment obsolete
The Lord rescued us from our distress
And brought us out of darkness

In these times we cry unto the Lord
We expect him to calm the hurricanes
And staunch the floods

And needless to say
Destroy our enemies
He will turn dry ground into springs
Sow the fields
Plant the vineyards
And yield fruits of increase
Setteth he the poor on high
The righteous shall see it and rejoice

This we expect
And cry out to the Lord

And still we wander in the wilderness

And still we cry upon the Lord

Psalm One hundred eight

1 My heart is fixed, O God;
I will sing, yea, I will sing praises, even with my glory.
² Awake, psaltery and harp:
I myself will awake right early.
³ I will give thanks unto thee, O God, among the peoples;
And I will sing praises unto thee among the nations.
⁴ For thy loving kindness is great above the heavens;
And thy truth reacheth unto the skies.
⁵ Be thou exalted, O God, above the heavens,
And thy glory above all the earth.
⁶ That thy beloved may be delivered,
Save with thy right hand, and answer us.
⁷ God hath spoken in his holiness: I will exult;
I will divide Shechem, and mete out the valley of Succoth.
⁸ Gilead is mine; Manasseh is mine;
Ephraim also is the defence of my head;
Judah is my sceptre.
⁹ Moab is my washpot;
Upon Edom will I cast my shoe;
Over Philistia will I shout.
¹⁰ Who will bring me into the fortified city?
Who hath led me unto Edom?
¹¹ Hast not thou cast us off, O God?
And thou goest not forth, O God, with our hosts.
¹² Give us help against the adversary;
For vain is the help of man.
¹³ Through God we shall do valiantly:
For he it is that will tread down our adversaries.

Wake up singing
And praise the dawn

Wake up laughing
And release the dead

Hear glory in the silences
Beyond the stars

Imagine light
Past gloom
Past night

Embrace the day
And bless the gods
Who have abandoned us

They are losing everyone
Who love them unawares

Such sorrow
And dismay

Psalm One hundred nine

1 Hold not thy peace, O God of my praise;
² For the mouth of the wicked and the mouth of deceit
Have they opened against me:
They have spoken unto me with a lying tongue.
³ They have compassed me about also with words of hatred,
And fought against me without a cause.
⁴ For my love they are my adversaries:
But I give myself unto prayer.
⁵ And they have rewarded me evil for good,
And hatred for my love.
⁶ Set thou a wicked man over him;
And let an adversary stand at his right hand.
⁷ When he is judged, let him come forth guilty;
And let his prayer be turned into sin.
⁸ Let his days be few;
And let another take his office.
⁹ Let his children be fatherless,
And his wife a widow.
¹⁰ Let his children be vagabonds, and beg;
And let them seek their bread out of their desolate places.
¹¹ Let the extortioner catch all that he hath;
And let strangers make spoil of his labor.
¹² Let there be none to extend kindness unto him;
Neither let there be any to have pity on his fatherless children.
¹³ Let his posterity be cut off;
In the generation following let their name be blotted out.
¹⁴ Let the iniquity of his fathers be remembered with God;
And let not the sin of his mother be blotted out.
¹⁵ Let them be before God continually,
That he may cut off the memory of them from the earth;
¹⁶ Because he remembered not to show kindness,
But persecuted the poor and needy man,
And the broken in heart, to slay them.

¹⁷ *Yea, he loved cursing, and it came unto him;*
And he delighted not in blessing, and it was far from him.
¹⁸ *He clothed himself also with cursing as with his garment,*
And it came into his inward parts like water,
And like oil into his bones.
¹⁹ *Let it be unto him as the raiment wherewith he covereth himself,*
And for the girdle wherewith he is girded continually.
²⁰ *This is the reward of mine adversaries from God,*
And of them that speak evil against my soul.
²¹ *But deal thou with me, O God the Lord, for thy name's sake:*
Because thy loving kindness is good, deliver thou me;
²² *For I am poor and needy,*
And my heart is wounded within me.
²³ *I am gone like the shadow when it declineth:*
I am tossed up and down as the locust.
²⁴ *My knees are weak through fasting;*
And my flesh faileth of fatness.
²⁵ *I am become also a reproach unto them:*
When they see me, they shake their head.
²⁶ *Help me, O God my God;*
Oh save me according to thy loving kindness:
²⁷ *That they may know that this is thy hand;*
That thou, God, hast done it.
²⁸ *Let them curse, but bless thou:*
When they arise, they shall be put to shame,
But thy servant shall rejoice.
²⁹ *Let mine adversaries be clothed with dishonor,*
And let them cover themselves with their own shame as with a robe.
³⁰ *I will give great thanks unto God with my mouth;*
Yea, I will praise him among the multitude.
³¹ *For he will stand at the right hand of the needy,*
To save him from them that judge his soul.

We have been bullied
Murdered

Robbed
By the armies of the night

Our enemies proliferate
They flourish in our sight

We pray to our ancestral God
The war god of the Canaanites
Our never-to-be-forgotten deity
That he render their offspring
Beggars and vagabonds
And crush them forever

Let extortioners obliterate their bank accounts
And barbarians cripple their troops

Let their posterity be blotted out
And the memory of them
Disappear forever from the Earth

As they loved cursing
Let them be cursed
As they loved killing
Let them be killed

Help us
O Lord my God
Save us
From those that condemn our souls

As we praise you
We await your mighty wrath
To visit our destroyers

We will go down together
Into the valley of darkness and blood
Suffocated by hatred and despair
In this way
We will understand
The overriding glory
Of the warrior

Our eternal war
No doubt
The meaning of life
Yes, Ma'am
Following your commandments
And your holy will

Amen

Psalm One hundred ten

1 God saith unto my Lord, Sit thou at my right hand,
Until I make thine enemies thy footstool.
² God will send forth the rod of thy strength out of Zion:
Rule thou in the midst of thine enemies.
³ Thy people offer themselves willingly
In the day of thy power, in holy array:
Out of the womb of the morning
Thou hast the dew of thy youth.
⁴ God hath sworn, and will not repent:
Thou art a priest for ever
After the order of Melchizedek.
⁵ The Lord at thy right hand
Will strike through kings in the day of his wrath.
⁶ He will judge among the nations,
He will fill the places with dead bodies;
He will strike through the head in many countries.
⁷ He will drink of the brook in the way:
Therefore will he lift up the head.

What is the meaning of power and might?
Will we require more wars
Reprisals
Detention camps
With us worshipping
Gods of wrath
Who teach us retribution
And revenge?

We have been told to judge ye not
As we sharpen our swords
Refine our arguments
And pray for victory

Do we even know our enemies?

In truth
Our adversaries are ourselves
Our nemeses
The very underside of us

We are the ones
We must learn to
Overcome

We are the ones
We need to forgive

We are the ones
Who need a better god

Psalm One hundred eleven

1Praise ye God.
I will give thanks unto God with my whole heart,
In the council of the upright, and in the congregation.
² The works of God are great,
Sought out of all them that have pleasure therein.
³ His work is honor and majesty;
And his righteousness endureth for ever.
⁴ He hath made his wonderful works to be remembered:
God is gracious and merciful.
⁵ He hath given food unto them that fear him:
He will ever be mindful of his covenant.
⁶ He hath showed his people the power of his works,
In giving them the heritage of the nations.
⁷ The works of his hands are truth and justice;
All his precepts are sure.
⁸ They are established for ever and ever;
They are done in truth and uprightness.
⁹ He hath sent redemption unto his people;
He hath commanded his covenant for ever:
Holy and reverend is his name.
¹⁰ The fear of God is the beginning of wisdom;
A good understanding have all they that do his commandments:
His praise endureth for ever.

Who made the world?
Was it a he?
A she?
Was it a thought?
Was it the imagination of the Universe
With its billion galaxies
Ten trillion stars
Uncounted suns and moons

And quadrillion light years?
Something like that—
Say what?

Were we made for worship
Or for wondering?

Were we the interplay
Of light
And mind
And love?

Why not live with that awhile
And see what happens?

Why not surrender
To our questioning?

Why not be still?

Psalm One hundred twelve

¹ *Praise ye God.*
Blessed is the man that feareth God,
That delighteth greatly in his commandments.
² *His seed shall be mighty upon earth:*
The generation of the upright shall be blessed.
³ *Wealth and riches are in his house;*
And his righteousness endureth for ever.
⁴ *Unto the upright there ariseth light in the darkness:*
He is gracious, and merciful, and righteous.
⁵ *Well is it with the man that dealeth graciously and lendeth;*
He shall maintain his cause in judgment.
⁶ *For he shall never be moved;*
The righteous shall be had in everlasting remembrance.
⁷ *He shall not be afraid of evil tidings:*
His heart is fixed, trusting in God.
⁸ *His heart is established, he shall not be afraid,*
Until he see his desire upon his adversaries.
⁹ *He hath dispersed, he hath given to the needy;*
His righteousness endureth for ever:
His horn shall be exalted with honor.
¹⁰ *The wicked shall see it, and be grieved;*
He shall gnash with his teeth, and melt away:
The desire of the wicked shall perish.

The President of the country club
Most definitely goes to church
And thanks the blessed God
For his success

Especially for
His Lamborghini
His Harvard MBA
And his portfolio

Unto the upright
Ariseth light in the darkness
That much is certain

He remembers to tithe
To give to the poor
And the capital campaign
That way
His righteousness
Will prosper
And endure

That's the plan

What about the rest of us?
Do we worship a replacement God
Or goddess
Depending
On the ghosts
That populate our dreams?

What do they expect from us?
What is the deal?

When will they tell us?

Better yet

When will we tell ourselves?

Psalm One hundred thirteen

¹ Praise ye God.
Praise, O ye servants of God,
Praise the name of God.
² Blessed be the name of God
From this time forth and for evermore.
³ From the rising of the sun unto the going down of the same
God's name is to be praised.
⁴ God is high above all nations,
And his glory above the heavens.
⁵ Who is like unto God our God,
That hath his seat on high,
⁶ That humbleth himself to behold
The things that are in heaven and in the earth?
⁷ He raiseth up the poor out of the dust,
And lifteth up the needy from the dunghill;
⁸ That he may set him with princes,
Even with the princes of his people.
⁹ He maketh the barren woman to keep house,
And to be a joyful mother of children.
Praise ye God.

What deity are we to praise
When the Lord
As he is called
Remains unknown to us
Especially in scripture
And mythology

Despite ourselves
Meaning
Our Masters degrees
Our PhDs

Our superior intellectuality
We are wired
To believe

Perhaps we are compelled
To praise the unknown god
To give him credit for everything good
And wonderful

He raiseth the poor out of the dust
Says the Psalm
He lifteth the needy out of the dunghill
Maybe so

Why go on pretending?

We live not knowing
Who we are
Or where we have come from
Except for the forest
And the trees

And the splendor of the night
Oh yes

The beauty of women
The roar of the sea
The music of the wind

The list goes on

It's better than theology

Isn't it?

Praise life

Psalm One hundred fourteen

1 When Israel went forth out of Egypt,
The house of Jacob from a people of strange language;
2 Judah became his sanctuary,
Israel his dominion.
3 The sea saw it, and fled;
The Jordan was driven back.
4 The mountains skipped like rams,
The little hills like lambs.
5 What aileth thee, O thou sea, that thou fleest?
Thou Jordan, that thou turnest back?
6 Ye mountains, that ye skip like rams;
Ye little hills, like lambs?
7 Tremble, thou earth, at the presence of the Lord,
At the presence of the God of Jacob,
8 Who turned the rock into a pool of water,
The flint into a fountain of waters.

With the God
We claim to know
We have become invincible
Pushing back oceans
Leveling mountaintops
And tribes

At all costs
Establishing Earth
As our domain

We have arisen from a bewilderment of deities
And found the fire
To incinerate doubt
And too much questioning

About the one
Everlasting
And absolute
Veracity

So help me God

So there

Psalm One hundred fifteen

1 Not unto us, O God, not unto us,
But unto thy name give glory,
For thy loving kindness, and for thy truth's sake.
² Wherefore should the nations say,
Where is now their God?
³ But our God is in the heavens:
He hath done whatsoever he pleased.
⁴ Their idols are silver and gold,
The work of men's hands.
⁵ They have mouths, but they speak not;
Eyes have they, but they see not;
⁶ They have ears, but they hear not;
Noses have they, but they smell not;
⁷ They have hands, but they handle not;
Feet have they, but they walk not;
Neither speak they through their throat.
⁸ They that make them shall be like unto them;
Yea, every one that trusteth in them.
⁹ O Israel, trust thou in God:
He is their help and their shield.
¹⁰ O house of Aaron, trust ye in God:
He is their help and their shield.
¹¹ Ye that fear God, trust in God:
He is their help and their shield.
¹² God hath been mindful of us; he will bless us:
He will bless the house of Israel;
He will bless the house of Aaron.
¹³ He will bless them that fear God,
Both small and great.
¹⁴ God increase you more and more,
You and your children.
¹⁵ Blessed are ye of God,
Who made heaven and earth.

¹⁶ *The heavens are the heavens of God;*
But the earth hath he given to the children of men.
¹⁷ *The dead praise not God,*
Neither any that go down into silence;
¹⁸ *But we will bless God*
From this time forth and for evermore.
Praise ye God.

The dead praise not the Lord
They go down in silence
Says the Psalm

Yet on the far side of paradise
We hear singing
Sounds of praise
Cries of joy and jubilation
Souls alive with one another
And with their Beloved

We remain here
Moored in reason
Definite in doubt
Nonetheless
Worshipping idols of silver and gold
Portfolios
And 401ks

We have voices
Sure enough
But we communicate
Incoherently
Our eyes see yesterday
Our ears hear
Schizophrenic monologues
Hands touch inconsistently
We speak with ambiguity
Roses cease to smell

All the while
We are wondering
About the dead
Who go down silently

Except when they don't

Some of us are still alive

Psalm One hundred sixteen

*1 I love God, because he heareth
My voice and my supplications.
² Because he hath inclined his ear unto me,
Therefore will I call upon him as long as I live.
³ The cords of death compassed me,
And the pains of Sheol gat hold upon me:
I found trouble and sorrow.
⁴ Then called I upon the name of God:
O God, I beseech thee, deliver my soul.
⁵ Gracious is God, and righteous;
Yea, our God is merciful.
⁶ God preserveth the simple:
I was brought low, and he saved me.
⁷ Return unto thy rest, O my soul;
For God hath dealt bountifully with thee.
⁸ For thou hast delivered my soul from death,
Mine eyes from tears,
And my feet from falling.
⁹ I will walk before God
In the land of the living.
¹⁰ I believe, for I will speak:
I was greatly afflicted:
¹¹ I said in my haste,
All men are liars.
¹² What shall I render unto God
For all his benefits toward me?
¹³ I will take the cup of salvation,
And call upon the name of God.
¹⁴ I will pay my vows unto God,
Yea, in the presence of all his people.
¹⁵ Precious in the sight of God
Is the death of his saints.
¹⁶ O God, truly I am thy servant:*

I am thy servant, the son of thy handmaid;
Thou hast loosed my bonds.
¹⁷ I will offer to thee the sacrifice of thanksgiving,
And will call upon the name of God.
¹⁸ I will pay my vows unto God,
Yea, in the presence of all his people,
¹⁹ In the courts of God's house,
In the midst of thee, O Jerusalem.
Praise ye God.

Beyond the bright sky of mind
Beyond reason
And the dark side of the moon
Our Beloved
Overlooks our marketplace
Our souk
Our carnival
And pronounces it his

Hear hear

I am humankind
Incline your ear
O Lord
Death has gotten hold of me

Hear hear
I mourn the massacred
The sacrificed
The living dead

The birds no longer sing
Lullabies are long forgotten
Hear my lamentation
Liberate my eyes from tears
And my feet from falling
That I may walk in the land of the living
And return to you

Hear, hear

Psalm One hundred seventeen

1 Oh praise God, all ye nations;
Laud him, all ye peoples.
² For his loving kindness is great toward us;
And the truth of God endureth for ever.
Praise ye God.

We are awash in love
And do not know it

We breathe the air
And bask in light
With no particular thanksgiving
For the day
And the night
And the stillness within

We do not recognize
The fullness of Earth
The abundance of beauty
Everywhere around us

We pray O Lord remember us
Words handed down
From one generation
To the next

In truth
We are aware
Only of ourselves

When will we become mindful
Of the divinity within?

When?

Psalm One hundred eighteen

1 Oh give thanks unto God; for he is good;
For his loving kindness endureth for ever.
² Let Israel now say,
That his loving kindness endureth for ever.
³ Let the house of Aaron now say,
That his loving kindness endureth for ever.
⁴ Let them now that fear God say,
That his loving kindness endureth for ever.
⁵ Out of my distress I called upon God:
God answered me and set me in a large place.
⁶ God is on my side; I will not fear:
What can man do unto me?
⁷ God is on my side among them that help me:
Therefore shall I see my desire upon them that hate me.
⁸ It is better to take refuge in God
Than to put confidence in man.
⁹ It is better to take refuge in God
Than to put confidence in princes.
¹⁰ All nations compassed me about:
In the name of God I will cut them off.
¹¹ They compassed me about; yea, they compassed me about:
In the name of God I will cut them off.
¹² They compassed me about like bees;
They are quenched as the fire of thorns:
In the name of God I will cut them off.
¹³ Thou didst thrust sore at me that I might fall;
But God helped me.
¹⁴ God is my strength and song;
And he is become my salvation.
¹⁵ The voice of rejoicing and salvation is in the tents of the righteous:
The right hand of God doeth valiantly.
¹⁶ The right hand of God is exalted:
The right hand of God doeth valiantly.

¹⁷ *I shall not die, but live,*
And declare the works of God.
¹⁸ *God hath chastened me sore;*
But he hath not given me over unto death.
¹⁹ *Open to me the gates of righteousness:*
I will enter into them, I will give thanks unto God.
²⁰ *This is the gate of God;*
The righteous shall enter into it.
²¹ *I will give thanks unto thee; for thou hast answered me,*
And art become my salvation.
²² *The stone which the builders rejected*
Is become the head of the corner.
²³ *This is God's doing;*
It is marvellous in our eyes.
²⁴ *This is the day which God hath made;*
We will rejoice and be glad in it.
²⁵ *Save now, we beseech thee, O God:*
O God, we beseech thee, send now prosperity.
²⁶ *Blessed be he that cometh in the name of God:*
We have blessed you out of the house of God.
²⁷ *God is God, and he hath given us light:*
Bind the sacrifice with cords, even unto the horns of the altar.
²⁸ *Thou art my God, and I will give thanks unto thee:*
Thou art my God, I will exalt thee.
²⁹ *Oh give thanks unto God; for he is good;*
For his loving kindness endureth for ever.

What does it mean
His kindness endureth forever?
Does our soul know secrets
That escape our minds?
Do we know mercy
When we are beaten down
And ridiculed
Or worse
Ignored?

My good intentions
Laugh at me

I am like a slave
Where is my strength?
What is my purpose?
Yet I am not delivered unto death
Something persists
Something endures

Open to me the gates of righteousness
Says the Psalm

I see many gates before me
Many altars
Many gods
Most demanding blood and sacrifice
All wanting to control my heart

I pray now for salvation
That I may know the God to Come
The God of Love

Those are the words
The intention

Yes

Psalm One hundred nineteen

1 Blessed are they that are perfect in the way,
Who walk in the law of God.
2 Blessed are they that keep his testimonies,
That seek him with the whole heart.
3 Yea, they do no unrighteousness;
They walk in his ways.
4 Thou hast commanded us thy precepts,
That we should observe them diligently.
5 Oh that my ways were established
To observe thy statutes!
6 Then shall I not be put to shame,
When I have respect unto all thy commandments.
7 I will give thanks unto thee with uprightness of heart,
When I learn thy righteous judgments.
8 I will observe thy statutes:
Oh forsake me not utterly.

ב *Beth.*

9 Wherewith shall a young man cleanse his way?
By taking heed thereto according to thy word.
10 With my whole heart have I sought thee:
Oh let me not wander from thy commandments.
11 Thy word have I laid up in my heart,
That I might not sin against thee.
12 Blessed art thou, O God:
Teach me thy statutes.
13 With my lips have I declared
All the ordinances of thy mouth.
14 I have rejoiced in the way of thy testimonies,
As much as in all riches.
15 I will meditate on thy precepts,
And have respect unto thy ways.

¹⁶ *I will delight myself in thy statutes:*
I will not forget thy word.

ג *Gimel.*

¹⁷ *Deal bountifully with thy servant, that I may live;*
So will I observe thy word.
¹⁸ *Open thou mine eyes, that I may behold*
Wondrous things out of thy law.
¹⁹ *I am a sojourner in the earth:*
Hide not thy commandments from me.
²⁰ *My soul breaketh for the longing*
That it hath unto thine ordinances at all times.
²¹ *Thou hast rebuked the proud that are cursed,*
That do wander from thy commandments.
²² *Take away from me reproach and contempt;*
For I have kept thy testimonies.
²³ *Princes also sat and talked against me;*
But thy servant did meditate on thy statutes.
²⁴ *Thy testimonies also are my delight*
And my counsellors.

ד *Daleth.*

²⁵ *My soul cleaveth unto the dust:*
Quicken thou me according to thy word.
²⁶ *I declared my ways, and thou answeredst me:*
Teach me thy statutes.
²⁷ *Make me to understand the way of thy precepts:*
So shall I meditate on thy wondrous works.
²⁸ *My soul melteth for heaviness:*
Strengthen thou me according unto thy word.
²⁹ *Remove from me the way of falsehood;*
And grant me thy law graciously.
³⁰ *I have chosen the way of faithfulness:*
Thine ordinances have I set before me.
³¹ *I cleave unto thy testimonies:*

O God, put me not to shame.
³² I will run the way of thy commandments,
When thou shalt enlarge my heart.

ה *He.*

³³ Teach me, O God, the way of thy statutes;
And I shall keep it unto the end.
³⁴ Give me understanding, and I shall keep thy law;
Yea, I shall observe it with my whole heart.
³⁵ Make me to go in the path of thy commandments;
For therein do I delight.
³⁶ Incline my heart unto thy testimonies,
And not to covetousness.
³⁷ Turn away mine eyes from beholding vanity,
And quicken me in thy ways.
³⁸ Confirm unto thy servant thy word,
Which is in order unto the fear of thee.
³⁹ Turn away my reproach whereof I am afraid;
For thine ordinances are good.
⁴⁰ Behold, I have longed after thy precepts:
Quicken me in thy righteousness.

ו *Vav.*

⁴¹ Let thy loving kindnesses also come unto me, O God,
Even thy salvation, according to thy word.
⁴² So shall I have an answer for him that reproacheth me;
For I trust in thy word.
⁴³ And take not the word of truth utterly out of my mouth;
For I have hoped in thine ordinances.
⁴⁴ So shall I observe thy law continually
For ever and ever.
⁴⁵ And I shall walk at liberty;
For I have sought thy precepts.
⁴⁶ I will also speak of thy testimonies before kings,
And shall not be put to shame.

⁴⁷ *And I will delight myself in thy commandments,*
Which I have loved.
⁴⁸ *I will lift up my hands also unto thy commandments,*
Which I have loved;
And I will meditate on thy statutes.

ז Zayin.

⁴⁹ *Remember the word unto thy servant,*
Because thou hast made me to hope.
⁵⁰ *This is my comfort in my affliction;*
For thy word hath quickened me.
⁵¹ *The proud have had me greatly in derision:*
Yet have I not swerved from thy law.
⁵² *I have remembered thine ordinances of old, O God,*
And have comforted myself.
⁵³ *Hot indignation hath taken hold upon me,*
Because of the wicked that forsake thy law.
⁵⁴ *Thy statutes have been my songs*
In the house of my pilgrimage.
⁵⁵ *I have remembered thy name, O God, in the night,*
And have observed thy law.
⁵⁶ *This I have had,*
Because I have kept thy precepts.

ח Hheth.

⁵⁷ *God is my portion:*
I have said that I would observe thy words.
⁵⁸ *I entreated thy favor with my whole heart:*
Be merciful unto me according to thy word.
⁵⁹ *I thought on my ways,*
And turned my feet unto thy testimonies.
⁶⁰ *I made haste, and delayed not,*
To observe thy commandments.
⁶¹ *The cords of the wicked have wrapped me round;*
But I have not forgotten thy law.

⁶² *At midnight I will rise to give thanks unto thee*
Because of thy righteous ordinances.
⁶³ *I am a companion of all them that fear thee,*
And of them that observe thy precepts.
⁶⁴ *The earth, O God, is full of thy loving kindness:*
Teach me thy statutes.

ט *Teth.*

⁶⁵ *Thou hast dealt well with thy servant,*
O God, according unto thy word.
⁶⁶ *Teach me good judgment and knowledge;*
For I have believed in thy commandments.
⁶⁷ *Before I was afflicted I went astray;*
But now I observe thy word.
⁶⁸ *Thou art good, and doest good;*
Teach me thy statutes.
⁶⁹ *The proud have forged a lie against me:*
With my whole heart will I keep thy precepts.
⁷⁰ *Their heart is as fat as grease;*
But I delight in thy law.
⁷¹ *It is good for me that I have been afflicted;*
That I may learn thy statutes.
⁷² *The law of thy mouth is better unto me*
Than thousands of gold and silver.

י *Yodh.*

⁷³ *Thy hands have made me and fashioned me:*
Give me understanding, that I may learn thy commandments.
⁷⁴ *They that fear thee shall see me and be glad,*
Because I have hoped in thy word.
⁷⁵ *I know, O God, that thy judgments are righteous,*
And that in faithfulness thou hast afflicted me.
⁷⁶ *Let, I pray thee, thy loving kindness be for my comfort,*
According to thy word unto thy servant.
⁷⁷ *Let thy tender mercies come unto me, that I may live;*

For thy law is my delight.
⁷⁸ *Let the proud be put to shame;*
For they have overthrown me wrongfully:
But I will meditate on thy precepts.
⁷⁹ *Let those that fear thee turn unto me;*
And they shall know thy testimonies.
⁸⁰ *Let my heart be perfect in thy statutes,*
That I be not put to shame.

ב *Kaph.*

⁸¹ *My soul fainteth for thy salvation;*
But I hope in thy word.
⁸² *Mine eyes fail for thy word,*
While I say, When wilt thou comfort me?
⁸³ *For I am become like a wine-skin in the smoke;*
Yet do I not forget thy statutes.
⁸⁴ *How many are the days of thy servant?*
When wilt thou execute judgment on them that persecute me?
⁸⁵ *The proud have digged pits for me,*
Who are not according to thy law.
⁸⁶ *All thy commandments are faithful:*
They persecute me wrongfully; help thou me.
⁸⁷ *They had almost consumed me upon earth;*
But I forsook not thy precepts.
⁸⁸ *Quicken me after thy loving kindness;*
So shall I observe the testimony of thy mouth.

ל *Lamedh.*

⁸⁹ *For ever, O God,*
Thy word is settled in heaven.
⁹⁰ *Thy faithfulness is unto all generations:*
Thou hast established the earth, and it abideth.
⁹¹ *They abide this day according to thine ordinances;*
For all things are thy servants.
⁹² *Unless thy law had been my delight,*

I should then have perished in mine affliction.
⁹³ I will never forget thy precepts;
For with them thou hast quickened me.
⁹⁴ I am thine, save me;
For I have sought thy precepts.
⁹⁵ The wicked have waited for me, to destroy me;
But I will consider thy testimonies.
⁹⁶ I have seen an end of all perfection;
But thy commandment is exceeding broad.

מ *Mem.*

⁹⁷ Oh how love I thy law!
It is my meditation all the day.
⁹⁸ Thy commandments make me wiser than mine enemies;
For they are ever with me.
⁹⁹ I have more understanding than all my teachers;
For thy testimonies are my meditation.
¹⁰⁰ I understand more than the aged,
Because I have kept thy precepts.
¹⁰¹ I have refrained my feet from every evil way,
That I might observe thy word.
¹⁰² I have not turned aside from thine ordinances;
For thou hast taught me.
¹⁰³ How sweet are thy words unto my taste!
Yea, sweeter than honey to my mouth!
¹⁰⁴ Through thy precepts I get understanding:
Therefore I hate every false way.

נ *Nun.*

¹⁰⁵ Thy word is a lamp unto my feet,
And light unto my path.
¹⁰⁶ I have sworn, and have confirmed it,
That I will observe thy righteous ordinances.
¹⁰⁷ I am afflicted very much:
Quicken me, O God, according unto thy word.

¹⁰⁸ *Accept, I beseech thee, the freewill-offerings of my mouth, O God,*
And teach me thine ordinances.
¹⁰⁹ *My soul is continually in my hand;*
Yet do I not forget thy law.
¹¹⁰ *The wicked have laid a snare for me;*
Yet have I not gone astray from thy precepts.
¹¹¹ *Thy testimonies have I taken as a heritage for ever;*
For they are the rejoicing of my heart.
¹¹² *I have inclined my heart to perform thy statutes*
For ever, even unto the end.

ס *Samekh.*

¹¹³ *I hate them that are of a double mind;*
But thy law do I love.
¹¹⁴ *Thou art my hiding-place and my shield:*
I hope in thy word.
¹¹⁵ *Depart from me, ye evil-doers,*
That I may keep the commandments of my God.
¹¹⁶ *Uphold me according unto thy word, that I may live;*
And let me not be ashamed of my hope.
¹¹⁷ *Hold thou me up, and I shall be safe,*
And shall have respect unto thy statutes continually.
¹¹⁸ *Thou hast set at nought all them that err from thy statutes;*
For their deceit is falsehood.
¹¹⁹ *Thou puttest away all the wicked of the earth like dross:*
Therefore I love thy testimonies.
¹²⁰ *My flesh trembleth for fear of thee;*
And I am afraid of thy judgments.

ע *Ayin.*

¹²¹ *I have done justice and righteousness:*
Leave me not to mine oppressors.
¹²² *Be surety for thy servant for good:*
Let not the proud oppress me.
¹²³ *Mine eyes fail for thy salvation,*

And for thy righteous word.
¹²⁴ Deal with thy servant according unto thy loving kindness,
And teach me thy statutes.
¹²⁵ I am thy servant; give me understanding,
That I may know thy testimonies.
¹²⁶ It is time for God to work;
For they have made void thy law.
¹²⁷ Therefore I love thy commandments
Above gold, yea, above fine gold.
¹²⁸ Therefore I esteem all thy precepts concerning all things to be right;
And I hate every false way.

פ *Pe.*

¹²⁹ Thy testimonies are wonderful;
Therefore doth my soul keep them.
¹³⁰ The opening of thy words giveth light;
It giveth understanding unto the simple.
¹³¹ I opened wide my mouth, and panted;
For I longed for thy commandments.
¹³² Turn thee unto me, and have mercy upon me,
As thou usest to do unto those that love thy name.
¹³³ Establish my footsteps in thy word;
And let not any iniquity have dominion over me.
¹³⁴ Redeem me from the oppression of man:
So will I observe thy precepts.
¹³⁵ Make thy face to shine upon thy servant;
And teach me thy statutes.
¹³⁶ Streams of water run down mine eyes,
Because they observe not thy law.

צ *Tsadhe.*

¹³⁷ Righteous art thou, O God,
And upright are thy judgments.
¹³⁸ Thou hast commanded thy testimonies in righteousness
And very faithfulness.

¹³⁹ *My zeal hath consumed me,*
Because mine adversaries have forgotten thy words.
¹⁴⁰ *Thy word is very pure;*
Therefore thy servant loveth it.
¹⁴¹ *I am small and despised;*
Yet do I not forget thy precepts.
¹⁴² *Thy righteousness is an everlasting righteousness,*
And thy law is truth.
¹⁴³ *Trouble and anguish have taken hold on me;*
Yet thy commandments are my delight.
¹⁴⁴ *Thy testimonies are righteous for ever:*
Give me understanding, and I shall live.

ק *Qoph.*

¹⁴⁵ *I have called with my whole heart; answer me, O God:*
I will keep thy statutes.
¹⁴⁶ *I have called unto thee; save me,*
And I shall observe thy testimonies.
¹⁴⁷ *I anticipated the dawning of the morning, and cried:*
I hoped in thy words.
¹⁴⁸ *Mine eyes anticipated the night-watches,*
That I might meditate on thy word.
¹⁴⁹ *Hear my voice according unto thy loving kindness:*
Quicken me, O God, according to thine ordinances.
¹⁵⁰ *They draw nigh that follow after wickedness;*
They are far from thy law.
¹⁵¹ *Thou art nigh, O God;*
And all thy commandments are truth.
¹⁵² *Of old have I known from thy testimonies,*
That thou hast founded them for ever.

ר *Resh.*

¹⁵³ *Consider mine affliction, and deliver me;*
For I do not forget thy law.
¹⁵⁴ *Plead thou my cause, and redeem me:*

Quicken me according to thy word.
¹⁵⁵ Salvation is far from the wicked;
For they seek not thy statutes.
¹⁵⁶ Great are thy tender mercies, O God:
Quicken me according to thine ordinances.
¹⁵⁷ Many are my persecutors and mine adversaries;
Yet have I not swerved from thy testimonies.
¹⁵⁸ I beheld the treacherous, and was grieved,
Because they observe not thy word.
¹⁵⁹ Consider how I love thy precepts:
Quicken me, O God, according to thy loving kindness.
¹⁶⁰ The sum of thy word is truth;
And every one of thy righteous ordinances endureth for ever.

ש *Shin.*

¹⁶¹ Princes have persecuted me without a cause;
But my heart standeth in awe of thy words.
¹⁶² I rejoice at thy word,
As one that findeth great spoil.
¹⁶³ I hate and abhor falsehood;
But thy law do I love.
¹⁶⁴ Seven times a day do I praise thee,
Because of thy righteous ordinances.
¹⁶⁵ Great peace have they that love thy law;
And they have no occasion of stumbling.
¹⁶⁶ I have hoped for thy salvation, O God,
And have done thy commandments.
¹⁶⁷ My soul hath observed thy testimonies;
And I love them exceedingly.
¹⁶⁸ I have observed thy precepts and thy testimonies;
For all my ways are before thee.

ת *Tav.*

¹⁶⁹ Let my cry come near before thee, O God:
Give me understanding according to thy word.

170 *Let my supplication come before thee:*
Deliver me according to thy word.
171 *Let my lips utter praise;*
For thou teachest me thy statutes.
172 *Let my tongue sing of thy word;*
For all thy commandments are righteousness.
173 *Let thy hand be ready to help me;*
For I have chosen thy precepts.
174 *I have longed for thy salvation, O God;*
And thy law is my delight.
175 *Let my soul live, and it shall praise thee;*
And let thine ordinances help me.
176 *I have gone astray like a lost sheep;*
Seek thy servant;
For I do not forget thy commandments.

There is a place within me
Undefiled
That holds your presence
And addresses you

From the beginning have I sought thee

Hidden
Silent
With my undivided heart
Wondering if I was imagining you
Or if you were truly there

Daily I meditate on the precepts ascribed to you
I beg you to open thou mine eyes
That I may behold your wondrous ways

I am a stranger to the earth
My soul breaketh for the longing that it hath

You were once a lamp unto my feet
A light unto my path.
Where are you now?

Rivers of waters run down mine eyes
I am insignificant and despised
Yet I do not forget you
I cry with my whole heart

Hear me, O Lord

Psalm One hundred twenty

1 In my distress I cried unto God,
And he answered me.
² Deliver my soul, O God, from lying lips,
And from a deceitful tongue.
³ What shall be given unto thee, and what shall be done
More unto thee,
Thou deceitful tongue?
⁴ Sharp arrows of the mighty,
With coals of juniper.
⁵ Woe is me, that I sojourn in Meshech,
That I dwell among the tents of Kedar!
⁶ My soul hath long had her dwelling
With him that hateth peace.
⁷ I am for peace:
But when I speak, they are for war.

Deliver my soul
From the lies I tell
Promising people they're fabulous
Beyond beautiful
Headed for fame
When they're as ordinary
As barnyard cats

I say I'm for peace
Yet I take sides
On every issue
Polarizing salt and pepper
If need be
Waging war
Over restaurants
And tattoos

"What do you mean by that?"

Taking offense
Where none was intended

Make me an instrument of thy peace
Sounds wonderful

Doesn't it?

Psalm One hundred twenty–one

1 I will lift up mine eyes unto the hills:
From whence shall my help come?
² My help cometh from God,
Who made heaven and earth.
³ He will not suffer thy foot to be moved:
He that keepeth thee will not slumber.
⁴ Behold, he that keepeth Israel
Will neither slumber nor sleep.
⁵ God is thy keeper:
God is thy shade upon thy right hand.
⁶ The sun shall not smite thee by day,
Nor the moon by night.
⁷ God will keep thee from all evil;
He will keep thy soul.
⁸ God will keep thy going out and thy coming in
From this time forth and for evermore.

I will lift up mine eyes unto the hills
Too far away to see
From this flat flood plain on which I live

I lift up mine eyes at night
Peering into the blackness
Impenetrable
Silent
Imagining I see distant light
And music

Imagining someone like me
On the other side of evening
Imagining me here
Wondering if he too
Is a fool

Psalm One hundred twenty-two

1 I was glad when they said unto me,
Let us go unto the house of God.
² Our feet are standing
Within thy gates, O Jerusalem,
³ Jerusalem, that art builded
As a city that is compact together;
⁴ Whither the tribes go up, even the tribes of God,
For an ordinance for Israel,
To give thanks unto the name of God.
⁵ For there are set thrones for judgment,
The thrones of the house of David.
⁶ Pray for the peace of Jerusalem:
They shall prosper that love thee.
⁷ Peace be within thy walls,
And prosperity within thy palaces.
⁸ For my brethren and companions' sakes,
I will now say, Peace be within thee.
⁹ For the sake of the house of God our God
I will seek thy good.

Pray for the peace of Jerusalem
Peace be within thy walls
And prosperity within thy palaces

Our feet shall stand within thy gates
O Jerusalem
Waiting for you
To show the world
How the offspring of Abraham and Sara
Mohammed and Khadijah
Jesus, Mary, and Joseph
How about Buddha?
Confucius?
Quetzalcoatl?

Certainly Ganesh
Can laugh together
Prosper
Share food at the same table
And pray to the same God

The one that lives in all our hearts
Whether we know it
Or not

Next year in Jerusalem!

Psalm One hundred twenty-three

1 Unto thee do I lift up mine eyes,
O thou that sittest in the heavens.
² Behold, as the eyes of servants look unto the hand of their master,
As the eyes of a maid unto the hand of her mistress;
So our eyes look unto God our God,
Until he have mercy upon us.
³ Have mercy upon us, O God, have mercy upon us;
For we are exceedingly filled with contempt.
⁴ Our soul is exceedingly filled
With the scoffing of those that are at ease,
And with the contempt of the proud.

Unto thee do I lift up mine eyes
O thou that dwellest in my troubled heart

Every day
I see before me the chaos of the marketplace
And feel the condescension of the proud

My eyes wait upon the hope
That you will acknowledge me

Or is the more persuasive argument
That I must acknowledge you
Who breathes
Within my soul?

I hear the reasoning of those
Who tell me you do not exist
That you are but a fantasy
We have dreamed to deal with death

When according to the argument
We will disappear
Never to return again

Have mercy on me
Wherever you are
I am filled with doubt and confusion
Anger and despair

Behold a simple man

Amen

Psalm One hundred twenty-four

1 If it had not been God who was on our side,
Let Israel now say,
² If it had not been God who was on our side,
When men rose up against us;
³ Then they had swallowed us up alive,
When their wrath was kindled against us:
⁴ Then the waters had overwhelmed us,
The stream had gone over our soul;
⁵ Then the proud waters had gone over our soul.
⁶ Blessed be God,
Who hath not given us as a prey to their teeth.
⁷ Our soul is escaped as a bird out of the snare of the fowlers:
The snare is broken, and we are escaped.
⁸ Our help is in the name of God,
Who made heaven and earth.

God is on my side
You'd better believe it

If that had not been true
I would have been swallowed up
By armies of barbarians
Who would confiscate my life
Sure as look at me

If God had not been guarding me
I would have drowned a thousand times
In sin and subterfuge

I hide
I disappear

How else to say it?
I curl into a ball

God?

Please keep me safe

My soul is a bird in a cage
Trapped apparently
Unable to fly
Unwilling to sing

I have escaped the hunters
And paid a price

My help is in the name of the Lord

Isn't that what he's there for?

Psalm One hundred twenty–five

1 They that trust in God
Are as mount Zion, which cannot be moved, but abideth for ever.
² As the mountains are round about Jerusalem,
So God is round about his people
From this time forth and for evermore.
³ For the sceptre of wickedness shall not rest
Upon the lot of the righteous;
That the righteous put not forth their hands unto iniquity.
⁴ Do good, O God, unto those that are good,
And to them that are upright in their hearts.
⁵ But as for such as turn aside unto their crooked ways,
God will lead them forth with the workers of iniquity.
Peace be upon Israel.

Those that do good to others
Who are upright in their hearts
Paying fair wages
Open minded
Without bias regarding gender or race
Who do good to the elderly
The disabled
Those crazy in the head

They will inherit the earth

Isn't that it?

Or will they be the ones to be comforted?

Wait
Which ones will see God?

Who will visit Israel
Next year in Jerusalem?

For ours is the Kingdom of Heaven
One day at a time
For thine is the power

I can't keep up

Stop

We need to keep our wisdom straight

Psalm One hundred twenty-six

1 When God brought back those that returned to Zion,
We were like unto them that dream.
² Then was our mouth filled with laughter,
And our tongue with singing:
Then said they among the nations,
God hath done great things for them.
³ God hath done great things for us,
Whereof we are glad.
⁴ Turn again our captivity, O God,
As the streams in the South.
⁵ They that sow in tears shall reap in joy.
⁶ He that goeth forth and weepeth, bearing seed for sowing,
Shall doubtless come again with joy, bringing his sheaves with him.

The bottom line is laughter
Vaudeville
Orchestras
Standup comedy
Into the release of joy

Everywhere
Artists awash in color
Sopping hip hop
Hey

The expectation of surprise
Around every angle
And every bend
The subtext one of astonishment

This is the presence of God
Now we rhumba
Can can

Tango
Pirouette

What about the waltz?

Hotcha!

Psalm One hundred twenty-seven

1 Except God build the house,
They labor in vain that build it:
Except God keep the city,
The watchman waketh but in vain.
² It is vain for you to rise up early,
To take rest late,
To eat the bread of toil;
For so he giveth unto his beloved sleep.
³ Lo, children are a heritage of God;
And the fruit of the womb is his reward.
⁴ As arrows in the hand of a mighty man,
So are the children of youth.
⁵ Happy is the man that hath his quiver full of them:
They shall not be put to shame,
When they speak with their enemies in the gate.

Do not build your house on sand
Announced the prophet
Lest a sinkhole swallow you
And carry you quickly
To wynken, blynken and nod

Watch where you situate

The force of hurricane and flood
Notwithstanding
Fools and psychopaths
May land you in the evening news

Instead
Now you lay you down to sleep
That you may dream
Of fairies calling you

Come home
To laughter
And to joy
And only afterwards
Build your monuments

Psalm One hundred twenty-eight

1 Blessed is every one that feareth God,
That walketh in his ways.
² For thou shalt eat the labor of thy hands:
Happy shalt thou be, and it shall be well with thee.
³ Thy wife shall be as a fruitful vine,
In the innermost parts of thy house;
Thy children like olive plants,
Round about thy table.
⁴ Behold, thus shall the man be blessed
That feareth God.
⁵ God bless thee out of Zion:
And see thou the good of Jerusalem all the days of thy life.
⁶ Yea, see thou thy children's children.
Peace be upon Israel.

Abundance
Is the blessing sought
For those wounded by unwelcome gods

Deities feasting on retribution
And revenge

For all who come close to the edge
Of despair

Look for the light
Sitting at the bottom of the night
Beyond black holes
And disbelief
That live within our souls

Sometimes the darkness holds
For a thousand years
Until unexpected

Hurricanes of grief explode
Changing everything

Making light visible

It will shine for you in all your ways
If you but look

Psalm One hundred twenty-nine

1 Many a time have they afflicted me from my youth up,
Let Israel now say,
² Many a time have they afflicted me from my youth up:
Yet they have not prevailed against me.
³ The plowers plowed upon my back;
They made long their furrows.
⁴ God is righteous:
He hath cut asunder the cords of the wicked.
⁵ Let them be put to shame and turned backward,
All they that hate Zion.
⁶ Let them be as the grass upon the housetops,
Which withereth before it groweth up;
⁷ Wherewith the reaper filleth not his hand,
Nor he that bindeth sheaves, his bosom:
⁸ Neither do they that go by say,
The blessing of God be upon you;
We bless you in the name of God.

The wheel is turning
Vibrations rise
The laughter loud and bright
Haters no longer predominate
They are confounded by the light

Past conflagration
And genocide
Beyond
The dreary daily news
Accidental deaths and hurricanes
Murders
Floods
And opioids

The blessing of the birds be fast upon you
Swallows
Orioles
Even Ostriches
Penguins
Red tailed hawks
Ordinary incidentals
Isn't that the way?
All of them singing
Under the silvery moon
They bless us in the name of earth and sky
And sun

Amen

Psalm One hundred thirty

1 Out of the depths have I cried unto thee, O God.
² Lord, hear my voice:
Let thine ears be attentive
To the voice of my supplications.
³ If thou, God, shouldest mark iniquities,
O Lord, who could stand?
⁴ But there is forgiveness with thee,
That thou mayest be feared.
⁵ I wait for God, my soul doth wait,
And in his word do I hope.
⁶ My soul waiteth for the Lord
More than watchmen wait for the morning;
Yea, more than watchmen for the morning.
⁷ O Israel, hope in God;
For with God there is loving kindness,
And with him is plenteous redemption.
⁸ And he will redeem Israel
From all his iniquities.

Waiting for the bus
The subway's late
So too World War Three
How long till Elavil kicks in?
Waiting for the phone to ring
Beep beep

Killing time
The plumber's overdue
Waiting to be born again
Is that true?
And die again
Out of the depths
And you

Somebody better listen
Somebody better come
What happened to God Almighty
Gone with the wind
It's true

This world isn't working
I'm clearly overdue
I hear God's inside me
Knock knock
Hello? Hello?

What else is new?

Psalm One hundred thirty-one

1 God, my heart is not haughty, nor mine eyes lofty;
Neither do I exercise myself in great matters,
Or in things too wonderful for me.
² Surely I have stilled and quieted my soul;
Like a weaned child with his mother,
Like a weaned child is my soul within me.
³ O Israel, hope in God
From this time forth and for evermore.

At least I know
I'm nobody
To write home about

I've never unlocked the meaning
Of the Universe
Mastered multiple languages
Accumulated PhDs
Ferraris
Or pied-a-terres
In Paris, Rome, and Malibu

I know my ancient place
That of a child
Faltering
Inarticulate
Happy to be invited here
What say
Let the good times roll

In the meantime
I have surrendered
To the mere magnificence of you

In belonging I exist

The alpha and the omega
Of a piece
With everything alive

Nothing else matters

Nothing but you

Psalm One hundred thirty-two

1 God, remember for David
All his affliction;
² How he sware unto God,
And vowed unto the Mighty One of Jacob:
³ Surely I will not come into the tabernacle of my house,
Nor go up into my bed;
⁴ I will not give sleep to mine eyes,
Or slumber to mine eyelids;
⁵ Until I find out a place for God,
A tabernacle for the Mighty One of Jacob.
⁶ Lo, we heard of it in Ephrathah:
We found it in the field of the wood.
⁷ We will go into his tabernacles;
We will worship at his footstool.
⁸ Arise, O God, into thy resting-place;
Thou, and the ark of thy strength.
⁹ Let thy priests be clothed with righteousness;
And let thy saints shout for joy.
¹⁰ For thy servant David's sake
Turn not away the face of thine anointed.
¹¹ God hath sworn unto David in truth;
He will not turn from it:
Of the fruit of thy body will I set upon thy throne.
¹² If thy children will keep my covenant
And my testimony that I shall teach them,
Their children also shall sit upon thy throne for evermore.
¹³ For God hath chosen Zion;
He hath desired it for his habitation.
¹⁴ This is my resting-place for ever:
Here will I dwell; for I have desired it.
¹⁵ I will abundantly bless her provision:
I will satisfy her poor with bread.
¹⁶ Her priests also will I clothe with salvation;

And her saints shall shout aloud for joy.
¹⁷ There will I make the horn of David to bud:
I have ordained a lamp for mine anointed.
¹⁸ His enemies will I clothe with shame;
But upon himself shall his crown flourish.

Once upon a time
We swore to be compassionate
The intimation being love

After how many careers
And how many perfect and imperfect relationships
And friends and lovers now no longer speaking
Until they do
And then they don't

What are we looking for?

What happened to our simple joy
When life was just a musical comedy
Or at least a western
With John Waynes on white horses
And Indians on black
Carefully staged
By MGM
Or was it Paramount?

Turn not your face from me
I promise to be good again
To people who are poor
Ugly
Stupid
Clueless
And good again
Even to you
If you want me to

I know
I am—
Depending—
A skin deep
Phony baloney
Narcissist

You think?

That's my curse
And my ordeal
And I suppose
My bottom-line appeal
Except to you
Who knows me best

I'm speaking to you
The Presence within

In your mercy
Please remember me

Psalm One hundred thirty-three

1 Behold, how good and how pleasant it is
For brethren to dwell together in unity!
² It is like the precious oil upon the head,
That ran down upon the beard,
Even Aaron's beard;
That came down upon the skirt of his garments;
³ Like the dew of Hermon,
That cometh down upon the mountains of Zion:
For there God commanded the blessing,
Even life for evermore.

*B*ehold
How good and pleasant it is for brethren to dwell together in unity!
And sistren too
The so-called female equivalent

That is to say
Until an argument breaks out
Reasoning goes off the cliff
The butter burns
Discipline's deceased
And even sistren goes out of date

More to the point
Siblings separate
Brethren battle
Sisters commiserate
And atheists arise

Lordy
Lordy
When will we be one?

Bless us, your beleaguered
One and all

No, not even one

Psalm One hundred thirty-four

1 Behold, bless ye God, all ye servants of God,
That by night stand in the house of God.
² Lift up your hands to the sanctuary,
And bless ye God.
³ God bless thee out of Zion;
Even he that made heaven and earth.

Have a blessed day, they say
Blessed with a single syllable

Okay

Or two

Either way
Suit yourself
Blessed be and sanctified
Because it has to be
The day
Consecrated by the light
And the love we bring to it

Bless ye the day
Bless ye the night
Bless ye brothers and sisters
Cousins
And accompanying cats
And dogs
And everyone in between

Psalm One hundred thirty-five

1 Praise ye God.
Praise ye the name of God;
Praise him, O ye servants of God,
² Ye that stand in the house of God,
In the courts of the house of our God.
³ Praise ye God; for God is good:
Sing praises unto his name; for it is pleasant.
⁴ For God hath chosen Jacob unto himself,
And Israel for his own possession.
⁵ For I know that God is great,
And that our Lord is above all gods.
⁶ Whatsoever God pleased, that hath he done,
In heaven and in earth, in the seas and in all deeps;
⁷ Who causeth the vapors to ascend from the ends of the earth;
Who maketh lightnings for the rain;
Who bringeth forth the wind out of his treasuries;
⁸ Who smote the first-born of Egypt,
Both of man and beast;
⁹ Who sent signs and wonders into the midst of thee, O Egypt,
Upon Pharaoh, and upon all his servants;
¹⁰ Who smote many nations,
And slew mighty kings,
¹¹ Sihon king of the Amorites,
And Og king of Bashan,
And all the kingdoms of Canaan,
¹² And gave their land for a heritage,
A heritage unto Israel his people.
¹³ Thy name, O God, endureth for ever;
Thy memorial name, O God, throughout all generations.
¹⁴ For God will judge his people,
And repent himself concerning his servants.
¹⁵ The idols of the nations are silver and gold,
The work of men's hands.

¹⁶ *They have mouths, but they speak not;*
Eyes have they, but they see not;
¹⁷ *They have ears, but they hear not;*
Neither is there any breath in their mouths.
¹⁸ *They that make them shall be like unto them;*
Yea, every one that trusteth in them.
¹⁹ *O house of Israel, bless ye God:*
O house of Aaron, bless ye God:
²⁰ *O house of Levi, bless ye God:*
Ye that fear God, bless ye God.
²¹ *Blessed be God out of Zion,*
Who dwelleth at Jerusalem.
Praise ye God.

I wish I could believe
In a mighty god above all gods
A Chairman of the Board of Deities
A four-star god
Who slaughters evil kings
And smites the first born of enemies
Man and beast
Democratic
Cobra
Tea Party Republican
Anyone who disagrees
With his imperial decrees

That is to say
A serious
Careerist God

Everyone worships something
Right?
Money
Armies
Hollywood

Did I say presidents?

In the meantime
This God I'm waiting for
Will control the weather
And the Fed

I'm still waiting

Have I been misled?

Like most everyone alive
I don't appreciate
Nuance
Ambivalence
And
Too much incongruity

Praise ye the name of the Lord

Psalm One hundred thirty-six

1 Oh give thanks unto God; for he is good;
For his loving kindness endureth for ever.
² Oh give thanks unto the God of gods;
For his loving kindness endureth for ever.
³ Oh give thanks unto the Lord of lords;
For his loving kindness endureth for ever:
⁴ To him who alone doeth great wonders;
For his loving kindness endureth for ever:
⁵ To him that by understanding made the heavens;
For his loving kindness endureth for ever:
⁶ To him that spread forth the earth above the waters;
For his loving kindness endureth for ever:
⁷ To him that made great lights;
For his loving kindness endureth for ever:
⁸ The sun to rule by day;
For his loving kindness endureth for ever;
⁹ The moon and stars to rule by night;
For his loving kindness endureth for ever:
¹⁰ To him that smote Egypt in their first-born;
For his loving kindness endureth for ever;
¹¹ And brought out Israel from among them;
For his loving kindness endureth for ever;
¹² With a strong hand, and with an outstretched arm;
For his loving kindness endureth for ever:
¹³ To him that divided the Red Sea in sunder;
For his loving kindness endureth for ever;
¹⁴ And made Israel to pass through the midst of it;
For his loving kindness endureth for ever;
¹⁵ But overthrew Pharaoh and his host in the Red Sea;
For his loving kindness endureth for ever:
¹⁶ To him that led his people through the wilderness;
For his loving kindness endureth for ever:
¹⁷ To him that smote great kings;

For his loving kindness endureth for ever;
¹⁸ And slew famous kings;
For his loving kindness endureth for ever:
¹⁹ Sihon king of the Amorites;
For his loving kindness endureth for ever;
²⁰ And Og king of Bashan;
For his loving kindness endureth for ever;
²¹ And gave their land for a heritage;
For his loving kindness endureth for ever;
²² Even a heritage unto Israel his servant;
For his loving kindness endureth for ever:
²³ Who remembered us in our low estate;
For his loving kindness endureth for ever;
²⁴ And hath delivered us from our adversaries;
For his loving kindness endureth for ever:
²⁵ Who giveth food to all flesh;
For his loving kindness endureth for ever.
²⁶ Oh give thanks unto the God of heaven;
For his loving kindness endureth for ever.

Let us give thanks to the human race
My relatives apparently
Inherently, irrevocably good
And other adjectives

Or don't you believe it?

We have shown mercy a million times
To the wounded of body and soul
Despite cynics
Naysayers
Miscreants
Who would argue otherwise
We have taken responsibility for the earth

Or tried to

We have overthrown
Despots
Terrorists
Barbarians
And lighted up the evening sky

We have harnessed the oceans
Fed the hungry
Reassured the dispossessed

Still we wander in the wilderness
Looking for Eden
And in the meantime
We create the world we know anew

We give thanks to the indwelling Spirit
Who teaches us
Compassion and mercy and love

We give thanks
For Chocolate
Marzipan
And Johnny Walker Red

As good as it gets

Amen

Psalm One hundred thirty-seven

1 By the rivers of Babylon,
There we sat down, yea, we wept,
When we remembered Zion.
2 Upon the willows in the midst thereof
We hanged up our harps.
3 For there they that led us captive required of us songs,
And they that wasted us required of us mirth, saying,
Sing us one of the songs of Zion.
4 How shall we sing God's song
In a foreign land?
5 If I forget thee, O Jerusalem,
Let my right hand forget her skill.
6 Let my tongue cleave to the roof of my mouth,
If I remember thee not;
If I prefer not Jerusalem
Above my chief joy.
7 Remember, O God, against the children of Edom
The day of Jerusalem;
Who said, Rase it, rase it,
Even to the foundation thereof.
8 O daughter of Babylon, that art to be destroyed,
Happy shall he be, that rewardeth thee
As thou hast served us.
9 Happy shall he be, that taketh and dasheth thy little ones
Against the rock.

We do not forget
The sorrows of the human race
Our DNA rises out of the dust
Of prison camps
Hanging grounds
Hospitals
Crematoria

From one generation to the next
We continue the same songs
Never say die
Marching together
Mad About You
Sis-boom-bah
In celebration of the ones we love

We remember
The God we once believed in
He watched over us
And kept us safe
And loved us

My God my God why has thou forsaken me?

Psalm One hundred thirty–eight

1 I will give thee thanks with my whole heart:
Before the gods will I sing praises unto thee.
² I will worship toward thy holy temple,
And give thanks unto thy name for thy loving kindness
And for thy truth:
For thou hast magnified thy word above all thy name.
³ In the day that I called thou answeredst me,
Thou didst encourage me with strength in my soul.
⁴ All the kings of the earth shall give thee thanks, O God,
For they have heard the words of thy mouth.
⁵ Yea, they shall sing of the ways of God;
For great is the glory of God.
⁶ For though God is high, yet hath he respect unto the lowly;
But the haughty he knoweth from afar.
⁷ Though I walk in the midst of trouble, thou wilt revive me;
Thou wilt stretch forth thy hand against the wrath of mine enemies,
And thy right hand will save me.
⁸ God will perfect that which concerneth me:
Thy loving kindness, O God, endureth for ever;
Forsake not the works of thine own hands.

In the middle of silence
Lives the God I hardly know

I speak
He does not answer

I speak again
No echo
No reply

Yet, something there
Something

Present and accounted for
Saves me from despair

When I am drowning in the dark
Something inarticulate
Incoherent
Barely audible
Whispers

I am
Who am
Who are you?

Psalm One hundred thirty-nine

1 O God, thou hast searched me, and known me.
² Thou knowest my downsitting and mine uprising;
Thou understandest my thought afar off.
³ Thou searchest out my path and my lying down,
And art acquainted with all my ways.
⁴ For there is not a word in my tongue,
But, lo, O God, thou knowest it altogether.
⁵ Thou hast beset me behind and before,
And laid thy hand upon me.
⁶ Such knowledge is too wonderful for me;
It is high, I cannot attain unto it.
⁷ Whither shall I go from thy Spirit?
Or whither shall I flee from thy presence?
⁸ If I ascend up into heaven, thou art there:
If I make my bed in Sheol, behold, thou art there.
⁹ If I take the wings of the morning,
And dwell in the uttermost parts of the sea;
¹⁰ Even there shall thy hand lead me,
And thy right hand shall hold me.
¹¹ If I say, Surely the darkness shall overwhelm me,
And the light about me shall be night;
¹² Even the darkness hideth not from thee,
But the night shineth as the day:
The darkness and the light are both alike to thee.
¹³ For thou didst form my inward parts:
Thou didst cover me in my mother's womb.
¹⁴ I will give thanks unto thee;
For I am fearfully and wonderfully made:
Wonderful are thy works;
And that my soul knoweth right well.
¹⁵ My frame was not hidden from thee,
When I was made in secret,
And curiously wrought in the lowest parts of the earth.

¹⁶ *Thine eyes did see mine unformed substance;*
And in thy book they were all written,
Even the days that were ordained for me,
When as yet there was none of them.
¹⁷ *How precious also are thy thoughts unto me, O God!*
How great is the sum of them!
¹⁸ *If I should count them, they are more in number than the sand:*
When I awake, I am still with thee.
¹⁹ *Surely thou wilt slay the wicked, O God:*
Depart from me therefore, ye bloodthirsty men.
²⁰ *For they speak against thee wickedly,*
And thine enemies take thy name in vain.
²¹ *Do not I hate them, O God, that hate thee?*
And am not I grieved with those that rise up against thee?
²² *I hate them with perfect hatred:*
They are become mine enemies.
²³ *Search me, O God, and know my heart:*
Try me, and know my thoughts;
²⁴ *And see if there be any wicked way in me,*
And lead me in the way everlasting.

Can any one of us be known
Even by ourselves?

Who understands my musings?
Me?

Who has searched me?
Who has known me?
Who?

If I take the wings of the morning
And dwell in the uttermost parts of the sea
So says the Psalm
Like Icarus
I shall surely drown

If I make my bed in hell, thou art there
Behold
To see me burn

Or will darkness cover me
And will you see me then?

I am born out of the earth
Ashes to ashes and dust to dust
You are the God of the evening sky
The maker of the moon and stars

I am earthbound
You are light

Where does our horizon meet?

And when?

Psalm One hundred forty

1 Deliver me, O God, from the evil man;
Preserve me from the violent man:
² Who devise mischiefs in their heart;
Continually do they gather themselves together for war.
³ They have sharpened their tongue like a serpent;
Adders' poison is under their lips.
⁴ Keep me, O God, from the hands of the wicked;
Preserve me from the violent man:
Who have purposed to thrust aside my steps.
⁵ The proud have hid a snare for me, and cords;
They have spread a net by the wayside;
They have set gins for me.
⁶ I said unto God, Thou art my God:
Give ear unto the voice of my supplications, O God.
⁷ O God the Lord, the strength of my salvation,
Thou hast covered my head in the day of battle.
⁸ Grant not, O God, the desires of the wicked;
Further not his evil device, lest they exalt themselves.
⁹ As for the head of those that compass me about,
Let the mischief of their own lips cover them.
¹⁰ Let burning coals fall upon them:
Let them be cast into the fire,
Into deep pits, whence they shall not rise.
¹¹ An evil speaker shall not be established in the earth:
Evil shall hunt the violent man to overthrow him.
¹² I know that God will maintain the cause of the afflicted,
And justice for the needy.
¹³ Surely the righteous shall give thanks unto thy name:
The upright shall dwell in thy presence.

Am I supposed to hate them that hate thee
As my people did

Once upon a time
Worshipping you with scalps and severed heads?

Will not hate beget hate?
Jihad
Inquisition
Reformation
Counter Reformation
Our fabulous wars of religion
Is that how it goes?

Madness at the heart of Man
Insanity the norm

How long before the bombs fall here?
Before invaders shatter us
Obliterating even children yet unborn
Fire incinerating memory
Of elm and willow oak, red buds, wisteria, Jack Russells,
Mixed breed retrievers
And racoons
Pot pourri, face jugs, boiled peanuts, Makers Mark

Gone
Departed
Dead
Erased

Preserve us from sadistic men
Approaching to demolish us

Let them be cast into the fire
That they rise not up again

We beseech you

We pray insistently

Hello?

Psalm One hundred forty-one

1 God, I have called upon thee; make haste unto me:
Give ear unto my voice, when I call unto thee.
² Let my prayer be set forth as incense before thee;
The lifting up of my hands as the evening sacrifice.
³ Set a watch, O God, before my mouth;
Keep the door of my lips.
⁴ Incline not my heart to any evil thing,
To practise deeds of wickedness
With men that work iniquity:
And let me not eat of their dainties.
⁵ Let the righteous smite me, it shall be a kindness;
And let him reprove me, it shall be as oil upon the head;
Let not my head refuse it:
For even in their wickedness shall my prayer continue.
⁶ Their judges are thrown down by the sides of the rock;
And they shall hear my words; for they are sweet.
⁷ As when one ploweth and cleaveth the earth,
Our bones are scattered at the mouth of Sheol.
⁸ For mine eyes are unto thee, O God the Lord:
In thee do I take refuge; leave not my soul destitute.
⁹ Keep me from the snare which they have laid for me,
And from the gins of the workers of iniquity.
¹⁰ Let the wicked fall into their own nets,
Whilst that I withal escape.

The ancestors watch over us
They guard our souls
They mind our hearts
They do

Ponder those you might remember
Ones who showed you kindness

Who listened
And taught you the meaning of love

Speak to them before you sleep
Tell them
If you are in trouble
We usually are
Ask them to help you

In their time they will answer you

Listen carefully

They do watch over us

They guard our souls

They do

Psalm One hundred forty-two

1 I cry with my voice unto God;
With my voice unto God do I make supplication.
² I pour out my complaint before him;
I show before him my trouble.
³ When my spirit was overwhelmed within me,
Thou knewest my path.
In the way wherein I walk
Have they hidden a snare for me.
⁴ Look on my right hand, and see;
For there is no man that knoweth me:
Refuge hath failed me;
No man careth for my soul.
⁵ I cried unto thee, O God;
I said, Thou art my refuge,
My portion in the land of the living.
⁶ Attend unto my cry;
For I am brought very low:
Deliver me from my persecutors;
For they are stronger than I.
⁷ Bring my soul out of prison,
That I may give thanks unto thy name:
The righteous shall compass me about;
For thou wilt deal bountifully with me.

I cried out to God
I had no one else
To care for me

No man or woman
Knew my soul

Grand opera in a little Southern town
Population seven thousand

Minus the escalating dead
A population on cabernet
And opioids
Glued to the NFL
And reality TV

In the meantime
Everyone prays
Make us great again
Great when Joe McCarthy
Terrorized the intellectuals
"Negroes" recognized their place
And women practiced how to smile

These days

People get poorer
Grass dries up
Ponds turn into sludge
Copperheads investigate
The neighborhoods

Carry my soul out of prison
I cry

Help me

Whatever it takes

Carry my soul

And I will praise thy name

Psalm One hundred forty-three

1 Hear my prayer, O God; give ear to my supplications:
In thy faithfulness answer me, and in thy righteousness.
² And enter not into judgment with thy servant;
For in thy sight no man living is righteous.
³ For the enemy hath persecuted my soul;
He hath smitten my life down to the ground:
He hath made me to dwell in dark places,
As those that have been long dead.
⁴ Therefore is my spirit overwhelmed within me;
My heart within me is desolate.
⁵ I remember the days of old;
I meditate on all thy doings;
I muse on the work of thy hands.
⁶ I spread forth my hands unto thee:
My soul thirsteth after thee, as a weary land. Selah
⁷ Make haste to answer me, O God; my spirit faileth:
Hide not thy face from me,
Lest I become like them that go down into the pit.
⁸ Cause me to hear thy loving kindness in the morning;
For in thee do I trust:
Cause me to know the way wherein I should walk;
For I lift up my soul unto thee.
⁹ Deliver me, O God, from mine enemies:
I flee unto thee to hide me.
¹⁰ Teach me to do thy will;
For thou art my God:
Thy Spirit is good;
Lead me in the land of uprightness.
¹¹ Quicken me, O God, for thy name's sake:
In thy righteousness bring my soul out of trouble.
¹² And in thy loving kindness cut off mine enemies,
And destroy all them that afflict my soul;
For I am thy servant.

Sometimes
The so-called enemy
Is just the emptiness of day

Otherwise it's mostly me

Imagination brings to mind
Memories
Of chemotherapy and death
Maybe my own
Insults hurled at the guilty
And of course the innocent

Why did I say that?

Behold the inner voices
informing me
I'm second-rate in stocks and bonds
Career
Shag
Imagine that
Keeping orchids alive
The occasional orgy
Just kidding
Maybe not

What is the so-called Lord
Everybody's famous Father God
Supposed to say about the ordinary life?

Hear me speedily, O Lord
Lest I be like unto them that go down into the pit
To survive on opioids
And phenobarbital
And Makers Mark
And shit

Until I don't see anything
But night

And night
Beyond the night

So
Tell me
Tell me when you take a break

What about you?

Psalm One hundred forty-four

1 *Blessed be God my rock,*
Who teacheth my hands to war,
And my fingers to fight:
² *My loving kindness, and my fortress,*
My high tower, and my deliverer;
My shield, and he in whom I take refuge;
Who subdueth my people under me.
³ *God, what is man, that thou takest knowledge of him?*
Or the son of man, that thou makest account of him?
⁴ *Man is like to vanity:*
His days are as a shadow that passeth away.
⁵ *Bow thy heavens, O God, and come down:*
Touch the mountains, and they shall smoke.
⁶ *Cast forth lightning, and scatter them;*
Send out thine arrows, and discomfit them.
⁷ *Stretch forth thy hand from above;*
Rescue me, and deliver me out of great waters,
Out of the hand of aliens;
⁸ *Whose mouth speaketh deceit,*
And whose right hand is a right hand of falsehood.
⁹ *I will sing a new song unto thee, O God:*
Upon a psaltery of ten strings will I sing praises unto thee.
¹⁰ *Thou art he that giveth salvation unto kings;*
Who rescueth David his servant from the hurtful sword.
¹¹ *Rescue me, and deliver me out of the hand of aliens,*
Whose mouth speaketh deceit,
And whose right hand is a right hand of falsehood.
¹² *When our sons shall be as plants grown up in their youth,*
And our daughters as corner-stones hewn after the fashion of a palace;
¹³ *When our garners are full, affording all manner of store,*
And our sheep bring forth thousands and ten thousands in our fields;
¹⁴ *When our oxen are well laden;*

When there is no breaking in, and no going forth,
And no outcry in our streets:
¹⁵ Happy is the people that is in such a case;
Yea, happy is the people whose God is God.

When I'm strong
Where does my strength come from?

When I sing, from whence the song?
Who teaches me to fight?

Where did I learn to walk
A straight and narrow path
To see that I am part of a greater whole
To understand it's not about me
Not just about me
But about everyone?

Who taught me to persevere
And to negotiate?

Deliver me from those
Who would demolish me
As soon look at me

Who exult in destruction
Who lie and steal

My days are as a shadow that passeth away

For now
There is a battle to be fought
A war to be won
With liberty and justice for all

God willing

Inshallah

Holy Mary

All of it

Amen

Psalm One hundred forty-five

1 I will extol thee, my God, O King;
And I will bless thy name for ever and ever.
2 Every day will I bless thee;
And I will praise thy name for ever and ever.
3 Great is God, and greatly to be praised;
And his greatness is unsearchable.
4 One generation shall laud thy works to another,
And shall declare thy mighty acts.
5 Of the glorious majesty of thine honor,
And of thy wondrous works, will I meditate.
6 And men shall speak of the might of thy terrible acts;
And I will declare thy greatness.
7 They shall utter the memory of thy great goodness,
And shall sing of thy righteousness.
8 God is gracious, and merciful;
Slow to anger, and of great loving kindness.
9 God is good to all;
And his tender mercies are over all his works.
10 All thy works shall give thanks unto thee, O God;
And thy saints shall bless thee.
11 They shall speak of the glory of thy kingdom,
And talk of thy power;
12 To make known to the sons of men his mighty acts,
And the glory of the majesty of his kingdom.
13 Thy kingdom is an everlasting kingdom,
And thy dominion endureth throughout all generations.
14 God upholdeth all that fall,
And raiseth up all those that are bowed down.
15 The eyes of all wait for thee;
And thou givest them their food in due season.
16 Thou openest thy hand,
And satisfiest the desire of every living thing.
17 God is righteous in all his ways,

And gracious in all his works.
[18] God is nigh unto all them that call upon him,
To all that call upon him in truth.
[19] He will fulfil the desire of them that fear him;
He also will hear their cry and will save them.
[20] God preserveth all them that love him;
But all the wicked will he destroy.
[21] My mouth shall speak the praise of God;
And let all flesh bless his holy name for ever and ever.

From one generation to the next
We are brimming
With the overflowing universe
of hummingbirds
And galaxies
DNA
Black holes
And Hollywood

What element holds this world together
With compassion indivisible
Mercy without end
Kindness as common as the sky

What factor
Overrides severed heads
And genocide
Slaughter
Rape
Insult to the indigent
Despite evidence that would argue otherwise?

Something perhaps that sings of love

Perhaps

Psalm One hundred forty-six

1 Praise ye God.
Praise God, O my soul.
² While I live will I praise God:
I will sing praises unto my God while I have any being.
³ Put not your trust in princes,
Nor in the son of man, in whom there is no help.
⁴ His breath goeth forth, he returneth to his earth;
In that very day his thoughts perish.
⁵ Happy is he that hath the God of Jacob for his help,
Whose hope is in God his God:
⁶ Who made heaven and earth,
The sea, and all that in them is;
Who keepeth truth for ever;
⁷ Who executeth justice for the oppressed;
Who giveth food to the hungry.
God looseth the prisoners;
⁸ God openeth the eyes of the blind;
God raiseth up them that are bowed down;
God loveth the righteous;
⁹ God preserveth the sojourners;
He upholdeth the fatherless and widow;
But the way of the wicked he turneth upside down.
¹⁰ God will reign for ever,
Thy God, O Zion, unto all generations.
Praise ye God.

Something in this world
Something indefinable
Wants to turn the wicked upside down

Still they continue
in their rampages
And deceit

Something wants to praise life
Beauty
And birdsong
The awakening spring
And birth

At least in fantasy
The blind see
The prisoners go free
The oppressed find comfort
And relief

We've been told not to trust in princes
Presumably that means
Money
And prestige

Something in this world
Something indefinable
Wants to put us back on track

Go with that something
However indefinable
However vague

That's a beginning

That's something too

Psalm One hundred forty-seven

1 *Praise ye God;*
For it is good to sing praises unto our God;
For it is pleasant, and praise is comely.
2 *God doth build up Jerusalem;*
He gathereth together the outcasts of Israel.
3 *He healeth the broken in heart,*
And bindeth up their wounds.
4 *He counteth the number of the stars;*
He calleth them all by their names.
5 *Great is our Lord, and mighty in power;*
His understanding is infinite.
6 *God upholdeth the meek:*
He bringeth the wicked down to the ground.
7 *Sing unto God with thanksgiving;*
Sing praises upon the harp unto our God,
8 *Who covereth the heavens with clouds,*
Who prepareth rain for the earth,
Who maketh grass to grow upon the mountains.
9 *He giveth to the beast his food,*
And to the young ravens which cry.
10 *He delighteth not in the strength of the horse:*
He taketh no pleasure in the legs of a man.
11 *God taketh pleasure in them that fear him,*
In those that hope in his loving kindness.
12 *Praise God, O Jerusalem;*
Praise thy God, O Zion.
13 *For he hath strengthened the bars of thy gates;*
He hath blessed thy children within thee.
14 *He maketh peace in thy borders;*
He filleth thee with the finest of the wheat.
15 *He sendeth out his commandment upon earth;*
His word runneth very swiftly.
16 *He giveth snow like wool;*

He scattereth the hoar-frost like ashes.
17 He casteth forth his ice like morsels:
Who can stand before his cold?
18 He sendeth out his word, and melteth them:
He causeth his wind to blow, and the waters flow.
19 He showeth his word unto Jacob,
His statutes and his ordinances unto Israel.
20 He hath not dealt so with any nation;
And as for his ordinances, they have not known them.
Praise ye God.

Somewhere
There is a God that knows the name of every star
And every asteroid
He's memorized
A billion galaxies

This God knows everyone by name
Every baby
Every broken heart

In the meantime
He is covering the earth with clouds
Preparing rain
Causing grass to grow
And wind to blow
And altogether
Forging peace

Theologians declare
This God is everywhere
On the ground
In the air
Alive in every intellect

Pardon me, Boy
Is this the Chattanooga Choo Choo?
How is that possible?

Damn
It's getting harder
And harder

To believe

Psalm One hundred forty-eight

1 Praise ye God.
Praise ye God from the heavens:
Praise him in the heights.
² Praise ye him, all his angels:
Praise ye him, all his host.
³ Praise ye him, sun and moon:
Praise him, all ye stars of light.
⁴ Praise him, ye heavens of heavens,
And ye waters that are above the heavens.
⁵ Let them praise the name of God;
For he commanded, and they were created.
⁶ He hath also established them for ever and ever:
He hath made a decree which shall not pass away.
⁷ Praise God from the earth,
Ye sea-monsters, and all deeps;
⁸ Fire and hail, snow and vapor;
Stormy wind, fulfilling his word;
⁹ Mountains and all hills;
Fruitful trees and all cedars;
¹⁰ Beasts and all cattle;
Creeping things and flying birds;
¹¹ Kings of the earth and all peoples;
Princes and all judges of the earth;
¹² Both young men and virgins;
Old men and children;
¹³ Let them praise the name of God;
For his name alone is exalted;
His glory is above the earth and the heavens.
¹⁴ And he hath lifted up the horn of his people,
The praise of all his saints;
Even of the children of Israel, a people near unto him.
Praise ye God.

Despite volcanos floods fires
Earthquakes hurricanes tornadoes
wars famine epidemics genocides cancer strokes
Keep going
Starvation
Alzheimer's
And malaria
What else?
Not to mention Murder 101
And occasional mudslides
It's a wonderful world
At least in the spring
To look at a budding apple tree
Emblematic of a world anew
Almost

The point of disaster might be simple enough
Despite everything else
It gives us an excuse to love

How else could one call the world wonderful?

Psalm One hundred forty–nine

1 Praise ye God.
Sing unto God a new song,
And his praise in the assembly of the saints.
² Let Israel rejoice in him that made him:
Let the children of Zion be joyful in their King.
³ Let them praise his name in the dance:
Let them sing praises unto him with timbrel and harp.
⁴ For God taketh pleasure in his people:
He will beautify the meek with salvation.
⁵ Let the saints exult in glory:
Let them sing for joy upon their beds.
⁶ Let the high praises of God be in their mouth,
And a two-edged sword in their hand;
⁷ To execute vengeance upon the nations,
And punishments upon the peoples;
⁸ To bind their kings with chains,
And their nobles with fetters of iron;
⁹ To execute upon them the judgment written:
This honor have all his saints.
Praise ye God.

Let us sing praises unto him
With the timbrel and the harp
The keyboard
And the steel guitar

Let us be joyful in glory
And sing aloud upon our beds
After intercourse of course
Are we alive or what?

Let the high praises of the Lord be in our mouths
A two-edged sword be smokin' in our hand

Settling scores upon the heathen
Meaning those who don't agree with us

From one generation to the next
When the economy goes off the track
When terrorists invade our streets
We will bind our kings with bankruptcy
And our nobles with fetters of iron
All written up
And written down
In the National Enquirer

We thrive on chaos
And much misunderstanding
Negative energy is better than none
In fact, we feast on it

Whatever else, God is on our side
He said so repeatedly

And lest we forget
The priests also wrote everything down

Here's to us!
There's none better

We're sensational

Amen

Psalm One hundred fifty

1 Praise ye God.
Praise God in his sanctuary:
Praise him in the firmament of his power.
² Praise him for his mighty acts:
Praise him according to his excellent greatness.
³ Praise him with trumpet sound:
Praise him with psaltery and harp.
⁴ Praise him with timbrel and dance:
Praise him with stringed instruments and pipe.
⁵ Praise him with loud cymbals:
Praise him with high sounding cymbals.
⁶ Let everything that hath breath praise God.
Praise ye God.

How do we praise the python?
Metaphorically of course

We don't really suppose
Snakes created the universe
Or do we now?

Yet, serpents sit silently
In the soul of each of us
Yes, they do
Waiting on prey
Speculating on survival at all costs

Spellbinding
Insinuating
Serpentine
Grace

If you can see them
For what they are

About the Author

Tony Scully is a graduate of Boston College and the Yale School of Drama. Several of his plays have been produced on and off Broadway. He is married to veteran Broadway actor Joy Claussen. In Los Angeles they both worked in the entertainment industry.

At Yale, he was a deacon at Battell Chapel under the Rev. William Sloane Coffin Jr. For five years afterwards, Scully was Project Director of the Jesuit-sponsored Woodstock Center for Religion and Worship at the Interchurch Center, 475 Riverside Drive, New York. Its mission: the exploration and renewal of liturgy in collaboration with leading anthropologists, sociologists, psychologists, and theologians. During that time, he also wrote a series of Prayers of the Faithful for Benziger Brothers, a liturgical press.

In his earlier career, for fourteen years Scully was a Jesuit in the Maryland Province of the Society of Jesus. During the seventies, Woodstock College, the Province school of theology, was affiliated with Union Theological Seminary in New York City.

In Los Angeles, in addition to writing for the entertainment industry, Scully directed The Return to Innocence Foundation, established by Garrett O'Connor MD and Fionnula Flanagan to deal with the multi-generational effects of cultural abuse in target populations.

After moving to Camden, South Carolina from Los Angeles in 2005, Tony Scully was elected Mayor of the city. He continues to write, direct, and serve as a theater and writing coach; he serves on boards of the region's arts and historical organizations.